TOXICOLOGY

Transform Your Unhealthy Relationships by Becoming Your Own Best Friend

S. Latria

DEDICATION

For my MiniMes Adina, Aniya, Brielle & Emery
Love each other as much as I love you.

CONTENTS

PART ONE:
SAFE SPACES

The safest place to exist,
The only place you'll thrive,
Is within your truth.

INTRODUCTION

Everywhere you turn, the word *toxic* is being thrown around like a hot potato that no one wants to be caught holding when the music ends. It's the elephant that we are no longer ignoring, but we also are not asking it to leave the room.

But I'm going to tell you the truth ladies: we can all be toxic. And that is okay because that doesn't mean we aren't also amazing. As people and as a population, we are all flawed, but that doesn't mean we aren't also valuable. Admitting our problems isn't a declaration of inadequacy; it shows a willingness to own our shit. Individual shortcomings don't have to hinder our collective greatness, *if* we learn to understand and appreciate our unique community despite those imperfections.

Before you ask, no, I am not a psychologist, psychiatrist, or doctor of any kind. I didn't even major in psychology or sociology in college, outside of one quarter my freshman year. If you need statistics, graphs, and peer-reviewed research to understand human behavior, you are in the wrong place. This book is a conversation amongst friends figuring out how to live, laugh, and love more than we bicker, berate, and betray. This is about healing, and we are here to have some much-needed girl chat.

For those who are bound to say the one opinion of a thirty-something-year-old woman cannot suffice as a valuable tool for all women, first I will say, *Ouch*! Here I am trying to do right by ya'll, and you're already doubting my ability and credibility just for the sake of being a dissenter. Secondly, I agree, somewhat. No one person becomes an expert on anything based solely on their experiences. I am aware of the limitation of one perspective.

In addition to the expertise I gained through a history of toxic relationships, I engaged with hundreds of women across every spectrum possible. Within those conversations, I absorbed, and we grew. Hearing universal underlying issues and concerns was therapeutic. I could relate to everything. Even if the direct situation did not resonate with me, how she felt I understood, or how she responded was something I'd also done. It reinforced how connected we are despite the infinite titles that separate us. This book is not about me or what I want; it is about what we need.

I hope you agree that any length of time is more than enough spent wallowing in sub-par relationships. A lifetime of entering and exiting toxic relationships will be a lot to unpack and put into its correct space. Don't waste time putting yourself together if you are content to unravel at the opposite end. To progress through your friendship wasteland, you must decide yesterday was the last day you were okay with living a toxic life. You're now making an agreement with yourself to not participate in unhealthy relationships, including with yourself. This decision is the most important one you need to make before proceeding. Commit now to becoming your own best friend, or don't continue.

You spend a sizable amount of energy on improving yourself through education, occupation, health, and love. As you advance through these quests for growth, doesn't it make sense to expend that same effort analyzing the relationships you navigate daily? How are you treating yourself, family members, and friends, in this moment? I started this book because I reached a point in my life where my friendships didn't feel like home anymore. I wasn't connecting with the women I loved and respected the way I did before. I didn't recognize myself in my actions and knew I needed to change. I decided to be the best friend that I could be and worked to figure out what that looks like in action.

This book will serve as starting point to begin your transition with assistance. You don't have to figure it out on your own.

Our community of women is comprised of the ones who help, love, and support us long before we find our significant other, career, or purpose. We use them as our audience to bounce ideas off of and absorb knowledge from before we step foot into a lecture hall or boardroom. These relationships are conditioning for life. Friendships between women hold so much understated value. Without the ceremony and the license, the hoopla of an engagement, or the benefit of a physical relationship, we declare to each other that we are soul mates, life partners, best friends... forever. It is time to feel the magnitude of that responsibility.

We need to look at why these relationships aren't working. Why does that BFF turn into just an acquaintance, or even worse, a sworn enemy? Is that dramatic? Yes. However, whoever has not gone from loving a friend to plotting inconceivable ways to ensure her demise, cast the first stone. Don't pretend you've never drafted a Kill Bill list. Whether or not you wanted to go full Beatrix Kiddo on her, somewhere along the way, it was decided that your relationship wasn't worth the effort anymore. But why? Who was most toxic to the relationship? Her, you, or both?

Chances are you had your first toxic relationship before you could spell toxic. Well, we are going to do more than spell it now. I am going to define, describe, explain, detail, and investigate that word, feeling, and experience until you understand its real-life implications. Toxicology is the study of the nature, effects, and detection of poisons. With this book, you will learn to identify where and how you can minimize the toxicity in your life. Doing so will improve your relationship with yourself and others. Being toxic isn't a social death sentence. It doesn't mean you are destined to be friendless. It means you need a little TLC. It means it is time to work toward YOU 2.0, the non-Beta, upgraded version.

If you're ready for that.
If you're committed to trying.
If you want to better to yourself, turn the page.

MY TOXIC STORY

To get the ball rolling, I'm going to share one of my most toxic relationships. Hopefully by being transparent, I will provide a connection between what I have gone through and what I am trying to achieve. My actions during the catastrophe of this toxic relationship and the clarity of self I was gifted in the aftermath played an important part in my growth. It helped me understand that I had to change as much as my relationships did. I was toxic, but I discovered I didn't like being that way.

I have had a friend since ninth grade. We were cheerleaders—kind of on the outskirts of the rest of the team—that banded together and became best friends. *NSYNC and a mutual dislike of a few squad members gave us the key ingredients to form a strong bond. With just enough similarities to keep us close and differences to keep things interesting, through the years of high school and into college we were still major players in each other's lives.

We both became so engrossed in the diverging paths our lives were taking that the dynamic of our relationship began to change. The daily texts and nightly talks gave way to weekly roundups and monthly visits. But with many miles, new jobs, schools, and relationships that didn't exist in high school separating us, we still felt satisfied with our current relationship. Or at least we made ourselves believe so. Looking back, that is when the first characteristic of toxicity, poor communication, started. The things we neglected to say led us to be blindsided by what was to come.

In retrospect, there were signs. Aren't there always signs? The indications of brewing discord had shown up years before. It wasn't as though we had a drama-free friendship. We had ups and downs like any other friendship. We made allowances and apologies to each other, and moved on. As I swept things under the rug and pretended as though our relationship had maintained the same quality, it left me little room to transition our friendship into the current context of my life. We were growing and maturing, but our relationship was not developing at the same rate. Funny how people always discuss establishing a strong foundation upon which to grow a stable relationship. We did that. But what is the point of making a sandcastle on top of steel? Slowly, it will still be weathered away regardless of how strong it started.

The thing that made this my most toxic relationship wasn't that we grew apart. It was along the unwinding I eagerly participated the toxicity redefining the relationship. I did not have the ability, or the courage, to address the issues within the relationship. When I had a growing annoyance with her inconsistency, I didn't communicate it. Instead of holding her accountable to being there for me, I dismissed her as unreliable. I accepted that not only was she not going to support me, but that it was okay for me to resent her for it. I was judge, jury, and executioner without even informing her of her Miranda rights or letting her know her charges.

I wish that was it, but it gets a lot worse. Feeling like I was "wronged" gave me the chance to be negative and mean, and I gladly took the opportunity. I allowed myself to become comfortable with discussing my gripes with her to other friends instead of to her. Sure, she knew that when she didn't show up to a party or event, I was upset. I wasn't completely mute. Still I knew she was mostly unaware of how hurt and disappointed I was. She didn't know I was purposely separating from her emotionally. How could she when I was constantly lying to her and telling her things were okay? I did not even give her the opportunity to meet my expectations because I didn't tell her what they were. Yep, more contradictory and confusing communication.

This was our new normal. While I resigned myself to maintaining the facade of friendship, my other friends encouraged me to discuss my issues with her directly. Smart friends they were. But I was so jaded by this point, I had convinced myself that she did not even have the capacity to be a good friend anymore. Not only was I doing myself a disservice by staying in an unhappy relationship, but I also wasn't even giving her a chance to be a better friend by being honest.

Although I am being extremely critical of myself now, it was not intentional back then. I wasn't telling her what my needs were in our friendship partly because I was still figuring it out for myself. I allowed for her to define the parameters of our friendship without my input and then despised her for not giving me what I wanted.

I was bad to myself and terrible to her, and I never took any of the blame. I was so focused on how she was letting me down that I completely neglected to admit I was being trifling and was more dedicated to being toxic than improving the health of our friendship. It took her planning her wedding, and us being forced to talk on a regular basis again, before I had had enough. Enough of her and enough of myself.

I did it. I had a candid conversation with her, including an apology, about the disaster that we had become. There were tears, admittance of fault on both sides, and a resolution to a new commitment to each other and to our friendship. It was a beautiful moment. I felt lighter and happier knowing that we were strong enough as friends to navigate through the last couple of years of bullshit and make it to the other side still connected. But before you applaud me too much, this is only the middle of the story. Unfortunately, the glow of our revitalized friendship lasted as long as a temporary tattoo.

Soon after I had been open and honest about what I needed from her and what I could afford to give, I was still left empty-hearted. Realistically, I should have been more patient for the newly decided transition to take place. I should have been more understanding that she was still in the middle of planning her wedding, which can put a strain on even the most non-toxic person. I did neither. I was too emotionally drained. I had waited too long hoping for reciprocation for me to wait now. I couldn't handle all the energy, attention, and care still being one-sided.

Despite my disappointment, because of the length of our friendship and the wedding coming up, I felt obligated to stand by her side. But my heart wasn't in it. I forced laughs, nodded my head in agreement, and kept making her smile, all while continuing to drag her name through the mud to friends whom I knew would sympathize. Toxic traits die hard, and I reverted with fervor. Only this time I allowed myself to completely justify in my toxic actions because I could tell everyone how hard I had tried to make things better. As her pseudo-friend, I counted down the days to her wedding and waited for my chance to escape with what little dignity I had left. Which I knew, at that point, was not a lot.

Where does that nonsensical mind set get you, you ask? Well, assaulting the cake at her bridal shower right before she is about to open her presents. You read that right. Bridal shower, week before the wedding, screaming, crying, and throwing my phone in the cake. Yes! Her maid of honor, me, went out with a *bang*! Without knowing it, I was reenacting a less comical scene from *Bridesmaids*. She said one small thing that by itself was not severe enough for me to explode. But it was just enough to set off the powder keg inside me that was just waiting on a flicker of ignition.

While sucking the frosting out of my phone and crying hysterically on my way home, it hit me. No matter how much she complained. No matter how unhappy she made me. No matter how frustrated I was with her for not being the friend I expected her to be, my actions were inexcusable. On a day that should have legitimately been about her, I made it about us. I matched her selfishness with a supremely selfish act of my own. I forced her to acknowledge the elephant in our friendship that had clearly not gone away. Instead of meeting her toxicity with rational thought, a plan of action, or a little compassion, I drowned her in my anger and out-toxified her like I was trying to win an award. There was no joy in my victory.

Soon after, we had another discussion in which I expressed, again, my lack of satisfaction in her ability to play a supporting role in our friendship. I told her that I felt there was no room for me in our "us." She briefly acknowledged this but then quickly switched to informing me of the jobs that still had to be done for the wedding.

It hurt, and it served as the final humiliation I could bear. I thought she would want me as far away as possible from any more cakes. No. She needed me, and that superseded anything that I had done or said. Did I help with the tasks? Of course, everything from the programs to making 200 cake pops the night before. After my performance, I owed her that much. We, or the lack of "we," annoyed me every step of the way. I still walked down the aisle, I danced, and I made a toast to the good times, all while harboring the toxicity within our friendship.

After that day was over, I vowed to never allow myself to experience that kind of negativity again. She wasn't perfect, but how did I let someone else's toxic behavior transfer and multiply in such a powerful way that, before I knew it, I was a monster? I had been a toxic, vengeful monster boozing it up to get through the ceremony and mentally rolling my eyes on one of the happiest days of her life. That's not the kind of person I am, but that was exactly the friend I had become.

How did this end? I told her I needed at least a month before talking to her again. After that month a few messages were exchanged, all initiated from her end. I felt bad about it; however, I had to place myself in a position of importance over her feelings. I checked out of the friendship. I did not allow her dependency on me interfere with the time I needed to reevaluate my role in the friendship and whether the time we had invested in the past would lead to more time into the future.

I didn't know if we would ever have anything that resembled what we once had. All I knew was, despite it all, I missed her so damn much. I would always love her and wanted beyond the best for her. At that time, it wasn't me. Until I was sure we could be the best for each other, I couldn't be an active part of her life. We both deserved that much. I missed her baby shower, I missed spending the holidays with her, and I missed the birth of her beautiful daughter. After being friends for most of our lives, I didn't hear her voice for over six months. It was one of the most difficult things I'd ever done, but detoxing is known to be a painful process.

We will all be toxic at some point. We will always deal with toxic situations and occasional hardships with the ones we love. But there is only one person who can make you toxic: yourself. Allowing someone's toxicity to permeate your life is just that—a decision, an occurrence you allow to happen. I couldn't let her toxic view of what our friendship should be to limit my ability to grow outside of it. The culmination of that chapter of our friendship led to the beginning of a new friendship with myself.

THE TOXIC R.U.L.E.

No one is more deserving of your love, appreciation and respect than you. If you're not starting with you as square one, your energy isn't being maximized, and your efforts are displaced. Don't be your own missed opportunity. We have all been told that when you point a finger at another person, you have three more pointing back. Therefore, before diving into the different toxic personalities and their effects on your relationships, you need to be willing to address these traits within yourself.

The Toxic R.U.L.E

Recognizing how you are toxic
Understanding why you are toxic
Loving yourself although you are toxic
Evolving beyond being toxic

Recognizing

Recognizing how you are toxic is the first step.

Recognizing is about honestly declaring a to-do list of characteristics you need change.

"I judge others by a different standard than I do for myself."

"I find it difficult to genuinely show excitement for other women's success."

"I need to be in charge of every relationship I participate in."

Think about it. Every day you use the mirror to get yourself physically presentable to interact with people. The mirror serves as your ally and enemy, highlighting the things you love and giving insight into the things that need a little help. Whether it is to boost your confidence or act as a gentle reminder that you have not been deep conditioning when you should, at some point in your day, you're expected to evaluate your reflection.

When was the last time you used the mirror to reflect on your actions and words? You think waxing is the most pain worth the effort, when it happens to be just the pain you are most comfortable with. Don't go through extensive effort to upkeep the one aspect of yourself that is bound to change, and not feel as comfortable assessing the internal aspects of yourself that need the most attention. We insist we are not the clothes we sport, the makeup we do or don't wear, or the heels that contort our feet into beautifully unbearable positions. Yet how often do you focus those outward accessories instead of your heart, mind, and spirit? It is time to criticize beyond your waist size and be okay with it. You cannot rectify your toxic traits if you refuse to recognize them. You want to check yourself before someone else has to.

If your botched, home dye job leaves you with an unflattering color combo, anyone who comes along and comments on your struggle strands is confirming what you already know. Just like those tragic tresses, you should identify your own toxic traits first. Outside opinion cannot define you, because you have already owned who you are. Although, this book is to detect and work on the toxic relationships you have, without an open and honest relationship with yourself, you have no hope of being a good friend to anyone else.

This first step will be extremely awkward and embarrassing. It must be. You may be seeing parts of your inner being that have been neglected for a long time. Traits that you have never seen as a problem will become blaring obvious as toxic. Take ownership of it. This is your toxicity. It belongs to you in all its ugly glory.

Becoming a more beautiful being requires you to bravely tackle the next part of the rule. After you recognize your toxic traits and write them down in your passion planner, you may try to immediately fix them. Who would want to declare themselves a danger zone and then stay that way? It is natural to want to jump to the resolution phase of your self-improvement. Don't do it. Growth happens in stages for a reason. It gives us the time we need to get fully acclimated to the new person we become. The second step is the easiest to dismiss as unimportant, but it is essential. I am positive that many will neglect this step, or rush through it and think all is well. All ain't well and won't be until you do the work.

Understanding

Understanding why you are toxic is the second step.

Understanding is where your previous toxic declarations turn into questions.

"Why do I feel uncomfortable that my friends have friends outside of our mutual circle?"

"When did I start prioritizing everyone else over myself?"

"What is it about seeing other people fail that makes me happy?"

"Why can't I express myself when I'm upset without resorting to yelling or cursing?"

When you go to the doctor, before you are diagnosed, they ask questions to determine what may have caused your ailment. They want to know what you have done to treat your symptoms so far, and they also ask if you are allergic to any forms of potential treatment. Once they have a diagnosis, they prescribe the needed medication or advise you of a course of action to begin the healing process. Sometimes the goal is to remove the illness or virus completely. Other times it is to implement a regimen for managing the ailment. Still, anything that is recommended is done with the cause of the illness in mind.

Congratulations, you have identified the specific strain of toxic you are dealing with! Now, why are you toxic? What makes you do the negative things you do? Understanding your motivation is how you get to the root of the unhealthy plant you grow from. You can cut the plant all you want, but until you determine the root of your issues, you will never have the tools to completely eradicate it.

Not understanding where your problems originate guarantees you'll ride that toxic cycle over and over again. Each time while circling, you believe you are making great strides, only to regress back to your previous state of mind. Every trip around that wheel will leave you more unsure that your toxicity is something you can contain or defeat. I wouldn't be surprised if you've already recognized your toxic traits well before reading this book but are still struggling to improve them because you lack understanding of yourself. Once you respect the importance of understanding your actions, you'll see the promise of change and actually see that change happen.

The difficulty of understanding lies in finding connections that may feel obscure or irrelevant. There are so many things that can cause toxicity; finding the source is more complicated than we anticipate. It will take time to investigate what triggers your toxic behavior. If you find yourself lashing out at your friends for seemingly no reason and regret it later, determine what is going on during those episodes that may set the scene for a toxic situation. You may pinpoint the trigger as being stressed at work. Although you may never know why your first response is to attack those around you, recognizing that you become a snapping turtle when you are under work pressure can give you a point of behavior to try to manage. Just knowing when it is safe, or optimal, to interact with your friends can save you a lot of self-loathing and repentance. Understanding the "what" arms you with the ability to figure out the "how" in making it better.

There will be trial and error along the way. All the answers you find while going through these two processes will aid you in the task of becoming less toxic, but even after knowing the answers, it will take time to incorporate them into your life. It is during that transition after acceptance and awareness—but before ability—that you will need to embrace the next portion of the rule.

Loving

Loving yourself, although you are toxic, is the third step.

Loving is when, while declaring your toxic statements and answering the difficult questions you've asked of your character, you stay grounded in correcting yourself instead of falling into self-condemnation.

"I need to apologize, but I also need to forgive myself."

"I had a better day today than I have had before."

"I'm proud of myself for pinpointing the moment I became unnecessarily aggressive in that situation."

Beyond self-care, which is an important practice that we discuss later, it boils down to, are you good to you? No amount of self-care can compensate for self-love. It's an *and* requirement, not an *or* option. Self-love and self-care share a symbiotic relationship. While they can exist independently, growth comes from their harmony.

If you complete the first two steps, you may feel as though you have beaten yourself up. During your internal review, you can take the analysis too far. Unless you are careful, you may find yourself a lot lower in confidence than you were when you started. Do not be unflinchingly or unnecessarily cruel to yourself along the way. You've done well, and relief is coming. While you are putting yourself through the ringer, part of the process includes purposeful loving—loving your toxic self enough to know that you may be flawed, but you will be okay.

You may be angry, saddened, or ashamed of things you have done and situations you have allowed affect your life for so long. I get it; no one wants to feel toxic. You're not alone. Think about the benefit you are doing yourself and everyone else around you by being brave enough to change. It won't happen instantly. You didn't gain all that toxicity overnight and you won't lose it in the time it takes you to read this section. But you will be armed with the tools to start shedding. Therefore, have some patience with yourself.

In my own toxic story, even when I was convinced I was becoming less toxic, cruising through my journey, and believing I was reaching the next level, I was humbled by my own toxicity. Need I mention again that I went full rage at a bridal party? It just doesn't get much worse than that. Even then, I didn't let that distract me from my ultimate goal. Although I retained a certain amount of remorse and shame surrounding those hideous actions, I didn't beat myself up over it. It happened. I was wrong. I need to grow. But I loved the fact that I could recognize that and that I still believed in my ability to become a better person. That is the kind of love you need for yourself throughout this entire process.

It is easy to discount progress. We often set standards that exceed reason, and then feel like failures when we don't meet those outrageous goals. Try not to set specific dates or inflexible requirements for yourself. This will be a lifelong journey, and you will probably never look in your inner mirror and say, "There is nothing left to do." If you're waiting to be toxic-free before appreciating the person you are, you are cheating yourself out of chances to celebrate all the milestones along the way. The fact that you are starting to walk this road is more than enough reason to increase self-love, which will give you the strength to persevere.

Being toxic is no different from being unhappy with another aspect of your life. If you want to lose weight, you don't throw in the towel as soon as you miss a gym day. If you are hoping to get into a stellar school, you don't decline other schools because you didn't get into one. If you want to be in a great relationship, you don't stop looking because a crush doesn't return your feelings. At least I hope you don't.

You struggle, but you believe. That belief helps you go the gym the next day, fill out another application, and go out with the cute guy you met in the coffee shop. Believe in yourself now. Love yourself today and tomorrow when your toxic level goes from a three to a seven. A little tolerance goes a long way. That is not just for other toxic people; it is also for you. Only once you feel like you may very well have loved yourself to death, begin the last part of the rule that will guide you through the duration of your own toxic journey.

Evolving

Evolving beyond being toxic is the next step.

Next, not last, because it never ends.

Evolving does not mean blind acceptance. It does not mean that you can be lackadaisical in your approach to greater emotional health. It means the exact opposite. It means aggressively addressing the toxin that infects you and not taking no for an answer, even from yourself. You do not use the comprehension of your toxic traits as a crutch to lean on, or as an excuse to permit them, but rather as the starting place to move from.

Evolving is surrendering to elevation over destination.

It is holding yourself accountable, answering questions about who you are, and smiling as you travel from your initial point A to your peaceful point B.

It is when you give up the need to stamp "done" on yourself and begin to ask, "What's next?"

Evolving is when you can say, "I'm still a work in progress," because you're actually working on that progress, not just because it sounds good.

Notice that I use the term *evolve* and not just *change* or *fix*. This is not an endeavor with a specific ending in mind; it is a continuous aspiration of development. Evolution is a natural adaptation—a biological progression that occurs over time in response to the environment in which you exist. You should want to be constantly evolving in your personal enlightenment. You aren't throwing a Band-Aid on a boo boo. You are altering your state of mind to transcend your current toxic state. You are redefining what is acceptable to give and receive from others. This is a fluid definition, able to be tweaked and tailored depending on where you are in your life and what you need to improve on at that time.

Evolving is the space where you use everything you have learned about yourself to upgrade your everyday. If you are willing to set a higher bar for yourself, imagine the expectations you will have for the other parts of your life. In addition to the rewards you will receive from making your inner woman healthier, by natural selection, you will be more inclined to associate with like-minded, healthy women. Having those women along during your evolution will encourage you to stay the path. If the strongest survive, smartly selecting your circle will arm you with the best resources to promote your chances of success.

While evolving, do not forget the tools that have gotten you this far. Continuously repeating them is only formula that makes it possible to move beyond stagnation. First, you recognized and owned your toxicity, holding yourself accountable for it. When you adopt a pet, you oversee their well-being and care. If you have a vicious pet, you may be required to keep them muzzled or far away from anyone until they are properly trained and socialized. Well, that's your toxic behavior. If you let that bad boy off the leash before you finish your personal obedience school, you must be prepared for those consequences and repercussions. You've officially adopted Lil' Toxie, and are now taking responsibility for its faults.

Second, you will be cognizant of your past and how it currently affects your present. You will use this information to modify your actions in your toxic future. Accept it now; you will have a toxic future. It is unavoidable, but improvable. Your goals should include focusing on remaining aware of your toxic-safe zones and when you are approaching a toxic meltdown.

Third, when you are having one hell of a time trying to figure out why you keep being so damn toxic, you will love yourself despite yourself. Becoming a better person is hard enough without worrying about not having your own support to get through the hard times.

Evolving gives you a grand amount of power that should cause you to rejoice. You have all the skills to lead a prosperous life that is as healthy as you want it to be. There are aspects of life you have absolutely no control over, but your inner woman is not one of them. She is yours to mold into something beautiful. That is your challenge that you inherit. You can't displace your issues on someone else or blame them for what you do.

Staying stationary is the equivalent of saying you are not worth the effort, when you are worth every effort. There is no purpose of continuing to climb any proverbial ladder if you have plateaued within yourself. As day by day and month by month pass, and you hold steadfast to the commitment to yourself, you will be grateful for having complete ownership of your emotional real estate. When you look at yourself and accept all that you are, you will appreciate that there is nothing that anyone can tell you, because you know and love it all already. You will analyze with care and advance with purpose. The R.U.L.E is your road map. Evolution is your ticket to the next phase of you.

PART TWO:

THE TOXICS

I am a Drama Queen-Persuader. I also tend to be possessive, jealous, and needy. Those attributes go hand in hand with my primary toxic diagnosis. In the past I have been an Enabler, a Love Enthusiast, and a Member of the Pack. Thankfully, they are no longer an issue. While those exact labels may not make sense now, they soon will.

"Toxic" is more than a personality. It is tone, speech, action, and emotion. It is behavior. While your individual methods of creating a toxic environment may vary, the effects are universal. Reading about these personalities will only be useful if you are willing to expose and correct yourself as much as you are looking to categorize others. Just because you have toxic behaviors and friends doesn't mean all is lost. While flipping through the chapters labeling the women around you, think about the quantifiable amount toxicity. Ask, "Is it a toxic trait?" Is it a toxic tendency that shows during stressful times? Do you have one toxic character flaw? Or are you dealing with a full-blown toxic personality?

This is not black and white. All of these labels exist on a full gray-scale. Successfully recognizing yourself and your community depends on your ability to appreciate nuance and the severity of those gray areas. However, to actively address these traits as a problem, you must call them out for what they are: toxic. Often the hardest part about getting through an issue is being able to identify, label, and discern why it bothers you. This section of the book is all about identifying who you are and whom you are dealing with. After you identify the problem, you can start the work of fixing it. Laugh a little at yourself, love yourself a lot, and grow piece by piece.

So, without any further ado, let me introduce our friends, co-workers, sisters, mothers... ourselves: the Toxics.

THE ENABLER

Toxic Tip: Be aware of not just what you allow, but what you encourage.

Her Toxic Scale: "Sure, I'll help you keep an eye on him online," to "Sure, I'll help you hide the body."

This is the most dangerous of all toxic behaviors for a few reasons.

1. It is the most prevalent toxic behavior.
2. It is the toxic behavior least likely to be considered toxic.
3. Without this toxic trait, all other toxic behavior would not exist.

We are *all* enablers. No matter how much you "keep it real," you, me, and all of us enable the toxicity within our friendships. It is easy to identify the issues within the friendship when it comes to pointing out what the other person has done or is doing. But asking, *If what she was doing was not okay, why did you accept her behavior?* is usually followed by a nine-month pregnant pause instead of a definitive answer. Your friendships work both ways. You cannot be in a toxic relationship of any kind unless you allow it. This is the primary way of enabling. So, you are responsible for continuously, consciously, and deliberately harming yourself.

You enable your way into bad relationships through your silence and participation every time you fail to call her out on her toxic shit. No one is perfect, right? Therefore, you don't expect your friends to be without their flaws. If you did, you wouldn't have any. You don't want to spend all of your time nitpicking. Not only would that be taxing, but it would open up the opportunity for them to return the favor. But if you know she is a scammer, and you knowingly accept the rewards from her latest efforts, stop pretending your pockets are not lined with dirty money. Stop hyping her up as the top of the class if you know she is most skilled in plagiarizing others. Stop acting like you don't know what will happen if she spends her rent money in Cabo. You knew as soon as you told her she should book the flight that she would end up on your couch. Own your supplemental actions as just as problematic as her initial behaviors.

Somehow you don't categorize the casual dismissal of your friend's negative behavior as encouraging it into existence. However, there is a line in which a genuine, normal appreciation of an imperfect person turns into a breeding ground for a seriously toxic relationship. That is the accountability that the Enabler neglects to assess when they thoughtlessly put their stamp of approval on their friends' actions. The things you don't do and say have just as much bearing on how your relationships function and whether they are healthy for all involved.

A Family of Enablers

Monica and her sisters all have a different relationship with their mother. Monica left the nest as fast as she could, while her sisters, Simone and Stacie, remained close to home. Their differing paths have impacted their levels of enabling, and there are many times when

Monica raises an eyebrow at the others' complicated dynamics. Her mother and sisters openly acknowledge they do things to enable their toxic patterns. Within their daily interactions, they knowingly promote behaviors that may not be in the other's best interest.

Monica's mother is known to talk to specific daughters about certain things. If she is mad at Simone, she will talk to Stacie, since Stacie will not analyze the reasons she is upset. Her mom knows if she talks to Monica instead, she will have to justify her anger and be asked to rationalize through it. Since that is not something she is always willing to do, she goes to the daughter she knows will enable her actions regardless of whether she is right or wrong.

If Simone says, "Sure Mom, there are a couple of bills due, but let's go shopping anyways!" it seems harmless until her cell phone is off and Monica needs to reach her. Simone knows what their mom is doing is not in her best interest, but she will still actively participate in the toxic activity.

Monica is no saint. She enables her mother when it benefits her as well. She spends hours planning things with her, getting so riled up with excitement that they cannot go to sleep at night. She knows that they tend to go more than a little overboard when presented with the opportunity to plan anything. They enable each other into this unhealthy state of to-do lists, completion logs, and trips to the Michaels store. Their mutual enabling means they feel completely justified when they wake up first thing in the morning to go to another store for more décor. Although Monica knows that her enabling is no better than her sisters', she is continues to do so because she needs her mother to enable her as well.

These are low level, less harmful examples of enabling. However, recognizing when you are enabling on a small scale will better help you see the trend and identify when it has become toxic. When someone is passionate about an opportunity, a new relationship, or even a new shirt, the last thing they want to hear is that it's a bad idea. We know this because it is true for us as individuals. It is easy to judge someone but hard to let them know you are doing so. Walking on the side of caution by avoiding too much criticism can instead lead to no criticism. There is a bold line between going out of your way to be judgmental or crass when informing a friend that something is awry and giving them a heads up as a good friend. We must become comfortable knowing we can make a choice to stand on the right side of that line, instead of avoiding it altogether.

The problem with enabling is not about encouraging your friend to go out with a guy even though you expect will not work out, because for all you know, they could prove you wrong. Rather, enabling is when you continue to encourage her after he proves to be emotionally abusive. At that point, you owe it her to let her know she deserves more. She may not take your advice into consideration, but have the fortitude to let her know when her actions or pursuits are damaging. It is when you consistently cosign with a friend setting herself up for failure that enabling becomes toxic.

Acceptable behavior is learned within social situations. When you enable someone, and allow their behavior to go uncorrected, you are giving them the seal of approval to continue those actions. Not if, but when, they show these same behaviors you have passively signed off on, can you really be upset by any negative backlash that may occur? Ask yourself what is more hazardous, the fire or the gasoline that continues to fuel it? When enabling, you may not be directly burning things, but you are the one fanning the flames. Decide whether you will be a fire starter or a fireman.

Silent Dissatisfaction

Azlan became upset with both Orin and herself when she silently enabled Orin's toxic behavior to define their relationship. If Orin abruptly dropped plans they had together in order to hang out with friends, Azlan never questioned it or asked for more consideration. Instead she returned the favor of her inconsideration in secrecy. When Orin later asked for a consolation hangout, Azlan would say she was busy although she was available. Passive aggressiveness became her new go-to method to feel like she had some form of retaliation against Orin's dismissive behavior.

The problem was, the only person who knew this was Azlan. Orin never saw Azlan's actions as a response of her own. As far as she understood, Azlan was just as busy and content as she was. Azlan was the only one suffering from her own poor communication.

Additionally, Azlan wasn't just enabling, she was also often flat-out lying. Instead addressing the issues that she had, she used them as ammunition and justification for her own toxic behavior. She found herself seeking more opportunities to stick it to Orin. She would no longer just be unavailable, she would be available, then cancel. Or she would ghost and not return calls and messages from Orin for extended periods of time.

Was Orin wrong for not prioritizing their friendship? Absolutely. But because Azlan didn't express her dissatisfaction, Orin was unaware that she was letting Azlan down. Instead of turning it into a learning moment and a growing opportunity, Azlan sought equivocation in an unhealthy way. All the while, she was still very much enabling Orin. Her passive aggressiveness was a small confidence boost that made her feel powerful against Orin's neglect. After enabling and sabotaging their relationship into a toxic mess, she only then understood she would have been better off actuating the power she really did possess: the power to communicate, the power the negotiate, the power to compromise, and, if all those failed, the power to walk away.

To ensure the correlation between 'witnessing' and 'enabling' toxic behavior isn't too abstract, let me apply it directly. You have the kind of friendships you want. So, if you have lackluster friendships, it is because you prefer them that way. Just like your toxic traits, your toxic relationships are yours to own. When you have a friend who consistently does not respect your position in the friendship, it is because at some point you allowed her to disregard you.

You may not have wanted to approach her actions then, or may not have even believed that those actions would continue, but still, slowly but surely, you allowed her to establish a pattern. The pattern could be talking over you until you don't feel you have a voice in your own friendship, negating your feelings until you don't feel comfortable expressing yourself, or not allowing you to equally participate in planning mutual events so your input does not have as much significance as hers. Somehow, you have given the impression that you are okay with how things are, and you have established a baseline of enablement that is toxic to both you and her.

How to Deal with Enablers

The first step is recognizing the enabler within. Self-control is the best defense an offense. Once you start to realize when you are enabling, you can slowly start to dial back those words and actions. When you have to address the enabling behavior of someone else, ask, *How do I deal with myself?* Knowing how you would want to be treated as your square one is the best way to approach a subject in a loving, kind, and, most imperatively, productive manner.

If you decide not to be an Enabler anymore and walk away from a toxic relationship that requires that of you, yay! You're on your way to a less toxic life. But wait, did you tell your soon-to-be ex-friend *why* you are walking away? If not, you are still enabling on your way out. It is not just the poor communication during the friendship that matters, it is also being quiet in your departure. You are still not saying anything about her actions and are therefore continuing to allow them to go uncorrected. Be real: you're not avoiding the conversation because you don't want to hurt her feelings. You are being silent because you don't want to be the villain. Putting your own comfort before the benefits of the confrontation makes you just as toxic as the situation you are attempting to avoid. That keeps you toxic long after the end of the friendship.

In addition to increasing your own toxicity by being selfish, you are denying your former friend the opportunity to grow. Without having a friend who has the strength to call them out on their ridiculousness, they do not get a firsthand, tangible account of how their actions affect their relationships. We can all be oblivious to the affects our actions have on other people. Sometimes we unconsciously hurt people because we don't put forth enough effort to not hurt them, not because we want to hurt them. Without social reinforcement from our closest confidants, relapsing or developing negative traits can easily occur.

As an enabler you make a choice. Before, during, and after a friendship, you decide whether you want to make a personal sacrifice to promote the betterment of someone else, or if you want to play along because it is easier. I urge you to choose the former. Especially if you have finalized your decision to move on from the friendship. If you compare what you have to lose by speaking up to her and what that woman has to gain by learning the impact of her toxic traits, you will see that good will once again overcompensate for the evil. At a minimum she will finally be aware that her toxicity does not go unnoticed and is directly affecting her life. Imagine how differently your entire relationship could have played out had you managed to just be brave from the beginning.

Dear Enablers,

This whole book is dedicated to you, to us, and to this momentous project of being the amazing tribe women we can be. Without our combined effort, nothing will change. Not us, not our relationships, and not our lives. I want you to feel like a superhero. The potential power we possess is way more dynamic than anything Marvel has yet to develop. The health of any thriving tree can be found in the quality of the land it is rooted in. We are that nutrient-rich, hydrated dirt. Everything that grows from it will be based off the strength of this initial admission: We have created and enabled our mess, so we are now charged with the responsibility to clean it up.

By reigning in this critical trait first, the quality of correction and enhancement you can have in everything else becomes limitless. That is not some hyperbolic phrase just to get you amped up, but feel free to get pumped. *Infinite* is the numerical representation of the amount of growth you can have. It is time to enable yourself and the people around you in a different way; it doesn't need to remain toxic trait.

I know this won't always feel like it is worth it. It is easier to just point finger and move on. However, I refuse to believe you wasted your hard-earned money to buy this book only to be turned off the moment you realize that it will put the onus of your development on your own shoulders. You knew that already. This is what you wanted. Your first toxic trait isn't anything that you can't manage. As you go through this book, and journey, the more you are open to see, the more you can change. Enable your progression.

THE LIAR

Toxic Tip: Let the truth set you free.

Her Toxic Scale: "I can barely notice that pimple on your nose," to "I can't come tonight, I'll be on a top-secret mission with B613."

It seems so cut and dry. Don't associate with people who lie. Case closed, on to the next toxic personality. Except there are so many definitions of what the Liar may be. The most obvious is someone who is generally untruthful. The kind of woman you can ask where she got her sweater, and she'll say she doesn't remember while holding the receipt for it in her hands. She's that lovely co-worker who doesn't own up to screwing up the shipment while standing next to you as your boss chews you out about it. Dealing with someone who has the ability, no, the audacity, to look you in the eye and lie to you leaves you asking WTF! It is one of the most frustrating and angering situations to find yourself in. Especially if it is done with no thought of how it might affect you. Like, c'mon sis!

Raise your hand if you've ever had a friend who had a looser grip on reality than most. You know that friend who has convinced herself she is significantly more important than she is and spends much of her time trying to convince the entire world of the same thing. She just got this promotion, was friends with this star, is about to purchase that major label purse, or just went on a date with someone who took her to the most expensive restaurant. All things that you know are barely truth adjacent. What do you find yourself doing? Playing into her fantasies and furthering her clouded perspective.

This is the point where most women say, "Oh I would never have someone like that as my friend, so I cannot be in a toxic relationship with them." Before you take that confident leap, think. Have you ever had a friend who tells you a guy was way into her and she had to get rid of him, when it is common knowledge she got dissed and discarded? How about that friend who is on that crazy lemonade and cayenne pepper diet with you, when she cheerfully updates you on her efforts while reeking of double cheeseburger? You're so hungry at this point, you can smell both patties on her breath, but she hasn't been cheating. These women are Liars.

So, you don't associate with anyone who is selective with the information they share when recounting a story? Often to make themselves look less guilty or more brave? You don't have one friend who always sets up hangouts just to cancel? You know no one who consistently shows up late or not at all? They are also Liars. It isn't just the woman who is untruthful in her words; it is also the woman who is untruthful in her actions. We give too much credit to intent and place not enough weight on the differing methods of deception. We can deny all we want, but we often allow our friends to get away with a certain amount of embellishment. If not addressed, it can give leeway to a very toxic situation.

The Only Flakes I Want Are Frosted

Alexandria has a friend, Rae, whom she can never completely rely on. They have a great time when they hang out, but, that is only if she actually comes. Rae is known to not attend events after RSVPing. Alexandria is annoyed by it, but she continues to associate with her. Because when it's good, it's good—and when it's bad, it's probably because she didn't show up.

Rae knows Alexandria is desperate to expand her audience for her podcast and could use her help with scheduling some of her connected friends. Alexandria didn't even ask, but Rae insisted that she knew just the right people who would love the opportunity to support and promote her show. When you are just starting out, the right interview can make you go viral and expand your brand overnight. This time Alexandria needed Rae to come through.

Whenever Rae confirmed a guest, Alexandria went through the process of prepping for the show. She spent hours researching information about the guest and potential topics for them to discuss. The success of this new business venture required her to be on top of everything; she wasn't going to come off looking unprepared or sloppy. When it came within days, or even hours, of show time, Rae would casually cancel. Everything from car troubles to double booking prevented every single one of Rae's people from recording.

Alexandria only marginally accepted the ridiculous excuses and half-assed apologies. She understood she needed to fully accept that Rae was never going to be dependable. Not in their friendship and not with her finances. She couldn't afford it personally or professionally to get her hopes up anymore and resigned herself to the fact that Rae probably never contacted or confirmed these guests on her behalf.

What Alexandria couldn't decide was whether it was because Rae just never made the time to follow through or if she didn't have the connections at all. Either way, Rae's ability to impact her business was over. Alexandria considered Rae a solid friend even when they were on shaky ground. She had interest in her beyond what she could do for her podcast. So why did she feel the need to set her up for failure when she didn't ask for her help in the first place?

Considering they shared so much before the podcast fiasco, Alexandria didn't know that to do with what was left of their friendship. Should she distance herself because the foundation of trust had been destroyed? Was Rae's inability to admit she just couldn't make it happen a reason to remove her from her life? Alexandria was lied to, and it created a toxic space in which a healthy relationship could not grow. Rae may have had good intentions, but her lack of honesty and execution has caused a wedge that Alexandria still isn't sure if she can jump over. We want to make our friends happy, even if it is temporary.

For some reason it feels better to make plans to hang and cancel than to just admit we can't fit them in our schedule. We want our friends to feel like they are a priority. So, we commit to do things that we know we can't, hoping by the time we must do them, by some miracle, we are able to make them happen. We hope the verbal declaration is enough of a gesture to excuse the physical letdown.

All of this is not okay, and we know it. We transition to bad Liars with good hearts instead of staying good friends. When people lie, their initial statement wasn't always untruthful. When they said they were excited to help you organize your new store, they really were. They may have just bit off more than they could chew, considering they already had important things lined up. Is that okay? No. They still were inconsistent. They still disappointed you. However, had they not lied to themselves initially, they would not have become a Liar to you.

Clock In & Clock Out

Katrina liked her new boss, Ophelia. Ophelia came into the office with the promise of maintaining a positive and productive work environment. Katrina thought Ophelia would be a great fit for the position and befriended her instantly. Meanwhile, Ophelia was smiling at the employees with one face and lying about them to her superiors with another.

When Ophelia condensed and reworded issues she brought to her bosses that had been already been discussed by the employees at length, Katrina still wanted to believe she was caring, even if not attentive. As time progressed, the perception of Ophelia within the office changed. Whispers of the inconsistencies within her actions and her statements became office chatter. Everyone in the office was on guard because it was hard to distinguish between those who were still Ophelia's allies and those who were aware of her toxic behavior.

Now Katrina, and all of her coworkers, operated in a constant state of dysfunction because Ophelia continued to operate dishonestly. Because of Ophelia's constant lying, people changed locations or lost their jobs completely. Katrina lost friendships as collateral damage to the disorder amassed under Ophelia's management. No one could be trusted anymore. Katrina felt her job now included not only the services she was providing the clients, but also ensuring she protected herself against Ophelia's campaign against the truth.

It became apparent the office was going to remain irrevocably damaged until Ophelia was no longer in charge. The only thing left for Katrina to do was to play nice and try to hold onto to her sanity until she was able to leave.

Liars rarely show their toxicity in the beginning. They will lull you into a false sense of security before exploiting your confidence in them. When the dynamics of the relationship change, you can be left confused. What happened to our co-worker who was always on top of everything? What happened to our sister whom we admired so much? Were the signs always there, or did things really change this much? Was she always a Liar?

The hardest thing about the Liar is knowing if you should stay committed to the person you believed them to be or accept them as is. Do you keep hope alive or accept you were wrong about them and move forward with that new revelation? You can get lost in the potential of the future instead of adjusting to the woman you have in the present. Her lies got you to this point, but why do you lie to yourself to stay?

How to Deal with Liars

When dealing with a Liar, it is important to make it known that you are aware of the truth. It removes the space that the Liar is comfortable in. When she says she'll definitely be there, remind her she's rarely there. Not to be rude, but to re-frame her confident affirmation and remind her that her current record is still in the red.

When she is unnecessarily boosting herself up, let her know it sounds like a stretch. She needs you to anchor her. The root of why our friends lie is so vast, there is no guarantee that they are doing it maliciously or to be intentionally deceptive. I have told people that I am fine, knowing that I felt one step away from the edge with the wind pushing behind me. It took them calling me out on it and confirming they knew I was lying for me to feel okay with sharing my struggles.

Embarrassment and pride can cause good friends to say and do untruthful things. They believe they are protecting themselves or us by over-sugarcoating or omitting important things. For these Liars, creating a safe space can provide the opportunity for them to be more open and truthful. Not all Liars are created equal. It is the severity and the consistency in which they lie to you that best determines the toxicity level you give their behavior.

For some Liars, being confronted by the truth is not enough to encourage them to acknowledge it. They instead become defensive or retreat. Somehow, facts with this type of woman can be adjusted, redefined, and ignored. If they cannot share the truth with themselves, in most cases, they have not, cannot, and will not be honest with you. This type of Liar will have a hard time removing themselves from the existence they are most comfortable in to ensure a healthy relationship with you. You can use your energy to overcompensate and repair the cracks that the Liar creates, or you can make that her responsibility and hope that she is able to rectify her mistakes. One of you will have to realign your priorities.

How deep does the rabbit hole go? There is a line between being a Liar and flat out delusional. If someone doesn't just detour from reality when it is convenient, but permanently resides in a location only they can find, Houston, you have a problem—a problem that you cannot fix. Walk away. Use Usain Bolt speed if you must. There is no saving a woman who cannot function in the real world. She must decide on her own that she wants to return. Engage with her from a distance, only when necessary, or when she cannot use her delusions against you.

Why am I so adamant that you should not participate in anything other than a surface level interaction with a delusional Liar? I stated earlier that when you are dealing with a Liar, chances are you end up lying a little as well, whether it is to excuse her actions or support her falsehoods. When you are dealing with someone who has a noticeable disconnect with facts, how can you exist within her realm and yours at the same time?

You can't. You will have to leave reality to play make believe with her. Playing pretend with her… is unhealthy for you. Your misguided attempts aren't helping her, and being okay with her reporting alternative facts proves you do not have her best interest in mind. Therefore, although I encourage, and hope, that you can use open communication to mend your relationship with a Liar, I advise you to be sure of exactly what kind of Liar you are dealing with. Their reasoning for lying, the depth of their deception, and whether they are noticeably lacking a grasp on reality makes all the difference between proceeding with caution and stopping with haste.

Dear Liars,

Tell the damn truth. Do you actually believe all the things you say, or are you just trying to convince everyone else? Whichever it is, stop. It isn't working. Anyone who has an investment in you right now will be turned off by your fringe association with accountability. If your friends do not just stop dealing with you, they may return the favor of lying and pretend they are still your friends when they've mentally checked out of the relationship.

Consider yourself fortunate if everyone around you has not already abandoned you. Because it is ridiculous to believe that anyone deserves to be lied to because you can't get your life together. However it isn't too late to change your course. Without even wasting time trying to remember all the lies you have told, all the events you've missed, and all the people you've let down, just start fresh today. If you need time to stroll back into the world of responsibility and accountability, opt for a Monday start. Just like that diet we all fail, the beauty is, if you mess up along the way, just restart the next Monday.

Keep trying until you get it right. I cannot stress enough that you are operating on borrowed time. Your actions will scream for you louder than the telltales you speak. So, get it together. Accept your limitations and embrace your possibilities. Not being forthright makes me think you are so uncomfortable being you. If nothing else, I hope that is a lie.

THE IMITATOR

Toxic Tip: Imitation is not always the sincerest form of flattery.

Her Toxic Range: "Can I wear that nail polish too?" to "Hedy from Single White Female."

You don't know who they are. Mostly because they do not know who they are. They mold so easily like Play-Doh, depending on the situation, it is hard for them not to reek of obsession. And I'm not talking about the nostalgic Calvin Klein fragrance. Unless you are a Persuader or a Bully, you will likely find yourself a little uncomfortable around an Imitator.

If you sign up for yoga, she is immediately doing Bikram classes. When you decide to be a lawyer, she is suddenly running for vice president of the Pre-Law Society. When you declare you'll be traveling in the summer, her passport comes in the mail two weeks later. Yes, she paid the extra to fee to have it expedited.

You have no idea if you have really good ideas, or if she just has none. It places a lot of weight on you when don't know whether your next plan will impact one or two people. Another indication that you are dealing with an Imitator is that she never comes up with a decision, even when coaxed. She's the person in your circle who waits to eagerly cosign whatever the group consensus is. Not one to go against the grain, Agreeable Annie will make sure her presence is complementary to whomever she is around.

Why she is toxic? Because a weak-willed woman can never benefit you in a relationship. What is she contributing if she brings nothing to the table? She is not just going with the flow, she is riding your coattail to success or destruction. Without her actively participating in the relationship, she is not giving you the true support or insight that friends provide. If you are driving off a cliff, you want friend who will make sure you press on the break, not rush to place her foot on the gas as well.

Double Re-Do

After college Amy was unhappy with her career aspects. Like many of her peers, her degree did not line up directly with where she saw her life going. Instead of sacrificing her potential happiness down the road by committing to a job she knew would never satisfy her, she made the brave leap to double down on her education and return to school for her second degree. Making the decision to start your educational career over is not one to take lightly. It requires an extension of the time and financial commitment you have already made once. Despite all these potential obstacles, Amy knew it was the only choice she had if she was ever going to accomplish occupational and personal satisfaction.

Much to her surprise, and mild annoyance, a close friend of hers, McKenzie, also decided that her current occupation was so displeasing that she too would be making the same drastic career change. Considering McKenzie graduated a year prior to Amy, was in a stable job in a different city, and had previously mentioned pursuing other unrelated career paths, she had more than ample time to come to this conclusion on her own. However, it was not until Amy had decided she wanted to go on this journey and had mapped out a specific path that McKenzie committed to trekking down that exact same road.

Having a friend by your side as you tackle one of the harder tasks in your life is an amazing asset. Amy did not want to discount the mutual support they could benefit from. But, she could not forget the times McKenzie wanted to go into other careers and social clubs in college whenever a mutual friend expressed interest in them. Did McKenzie really want to do this, or did she just want to do whatever someone else was doing? Amy was fully prepared to accept responsibility for her own choices, but she did not want the pressure of having to carry someone else's future fortune as well.

Truthfulness in representation is key. In our effort to establish a bond in a relationship, we can attempt to fit in with our new friend by downplaying our differences. That isn't to say that we completely deny our personalities, but we highlight the things we have in common, even if they are not our dominant traits. As much as the media would like you to believe that everyone is looking for a reason to be different, we still want to be accepted by others—even if it is only by the others who proudly declare themselves just as different. However, when you begin to mimic someone you want to be around in hopes that it will make you closer, that false portrayal of who you are is toxic.

The Confusion of Assimilation

It can be difficult to understand who your friend is if they drastically change their personality when their surroundings change. The Assimilator is the Imitator's first cousin. A woman who is sweet and endearing when you are together but switches into an overbearing Bully when she is around her CrossFit pals can leave you wondering which version of her is real. Is she pretending to be like you, or is she pretending to be like them? Don't confuse a Phony, defined in the next chapter, with someone who is desperate to assimilate. An Assimilator is someone who changes their personality depending on the people they are around to retain their friendships. Think of them as a conditional Imitator. They are not trying to deceive you specifically into a false friendship, although they come off as inauthentic at times.

As multifaceted women, different qualities of your personality will be more dominant depending on the dynamics of your friendship. That isn't unhealthy. There is a difference between showing different sides of yourself and different versions of yourself. Assimilators become toxic as people-pleasers in search of acceptance, regardless of whether it complements or aligns with their natural state. They manage to ensure their broadcasted qualities, authentic or not, can cover the largest span of women possible.

Assimilators act as though their chances of getting along are dependent on their ability to blend in. They operate under the impression that if they camouflage the parts of themselves that do not align with that specific group of people, their presence will be more appreciated. This includes the portions of their personality they are already comfortable sharing with you. Although they should work to show their complete personality more, the deception they are committing is inward as much as it is outward. They're overcompensating for their fear of rejection by committing to being everything everyone wants. That's impossible, but they haven't reconciled that within themselves. Before writing these women off, try to evaluate their intention versus their execution.

How to Deal with Imitators

Embrace their differences. Imitators try to be what you are for a couple of reasons. Primarily it is fear of the unknown. They have yet to figure themselves out. They do not trust that their instincts are accurate enough to follow. Therefore, the respect they have for you or their desire to have what you have makes you the perfect candidate for emulation. Instead of developing their own route to do so, they find it more efficient to just replicate your qualities or path, in hopes of reaching your success.

They also fear they are not good enough. Everyone has a personality no matter how plain. Imitators have convinced themselves that their flavor of life could never be palatable to anyone else, so they should adopt a new one to guarantee they will be welcomed. Their lack or self-awareness motivates them to abandon themselves and find a more assured source of completion.

Imitators are fumbling around, grasping at what seems like the most promising straws; try not to destroy the fragile confidence they have. Counterbalance their desire to copy you by congratulating their uniqueness. Chances are these women do not get encouraged enough. They do not get lifted in praise or reminded that their individuality is an asset they should capitalize on. Imitation has a lot to do with a lack of self-esteem. You are not personally responsible for repairing the bridge between them and self-confidence; however, it certainly does not hurt to be their cheerleader. The more you applaud these women when they branch out on their own, the more they will realize, and believe, that they are capable of successfully being themselves.

Dear Imitators,

Be yourself, and you will attract what you are. You clearly have not heard that you are good enough often enough.

Let me tell you now: You have always been good enough for love and respect, as you are. No changes required. You exist beyond the boundaries that you have built to protect you, and your world is waiting to meet you. The real you. Not the you that you think we want to see. And not the you that you have fashioned after the women around you.

If they are your true friends, they will accept you, just as you have accepted them.

If I am an alto and you are a soprano, do not lower your octave to match me. Your soul's voice is just as beautiful as mine. Harmonizing, not synchronizing, will create a better song. We will have moments when our differences create distance between us, but those same differences are what make us so powerful together. Should you meet someone along the way who tries to stifle the supreme being you are, instead of surrendering, ask yourself why they are so eager to try to diminish your magic. Don't let their fears threaten your value.

It's crazy that you are afraid to show your wings, and I am afraid that we will never get the chance to see you fly. I speak for all the women who love you when I say it would be a travesty to not see you soar.

THE PHONY

Toxic Tip: The math never fails. Positive or negative energy multiplied by a negative situation will always be negative.

Her Toxic Scale: Hair clip-ins to $25 Hermes sold on the street corner.

We have all been at an event where we are near someone we'd rather smack than smile at, and the situation dictates that we remain cordial rather than catty. Our personal grievances with other women can't always be treated as a public problem. When reputation is at stake, sometimes we must play nice by putting on our fake face to grin and bear it. That being said, there is no reason to wear that same fake face in friendships with those whom you are genuinely invested in. Phonies are women who willingly participate in inauthentic friendships.

A Phony's deception is intentional. This is what makes her supremely toxic. Often unwittingly, you absorb the risks of confiding in, depending on, or expecting authenticity from someone who is fake. Much like the Liar, the Phony is an illusionist. Unlike the Liar, the illusion extends beyond the definition of themselves and permeates the very construct of their interaction with you. If that sounds similar, it is because deception at the end of the day all feels the same. However, there is an important distinction between the Phony and the Liar. Remember, a Liar is untruthful with herself, about herself, and as a result, with you. A Phony is lying about being your friend.

I'll Take Anything

Meena sought out and committed herself to a friendship that didn't exist. She was so eager to have platonic companionship, she accepted an artificial connection with Indira although she knew it wasn't genuine. Her commitment was never her; Indira could have been anyone. She just needed to have a friend around to fill the void of the relationship she actually wanted. Meena wanted to be a positive mentor, or like a big sister to one of her peers, and Indira gleefully signed up for the position.

However, things between them weren't natural despite doing friendly things together. Instead of mutually beneficial, they were mutually used by one another. Indira took whatever she could from Meena without worrying about returning the investment, and Meena was okay with that.

Meena needed someone to influence, and Indira needing someone manipulate to take care of her. Neither was willing to admit that there was no real relationship outside of their unhealthy needs. Considering they were just going through the motions without any of the emotion, the upkeep of the false friendship proved tiring. When it became apparent that Indira could get nothing more from Meena, she stopped reaching out, effectively ending the relationship. Indira was being an Opportunist, capitalizing on what she could get, and Meena was a Phony because she was aware of her and Indira's intentions but participated anyway. Ultimately, she felt relief from no longer having to participate in the counterfeit friendship. The relationship with Indira never satisfied her initial goal of having a deep connection, and she shouldn't have tried to be content with just scratching at the surface.

Disclaimer: Violence is a big no-no! We shouldn't be fighting. Don't believe the hype of thrown punches and shattered glasses on television. We need to be able to use our words as mature teens or adults to solve our problems.

But! If you ever happen to be facing an altercation with a group of women and you're surrounded, you're outnumbered, you're afraid... would you rather have a ride-or-die friend by your side or the chick who would Facebook live you getting dogwalked from multiple angles? Do you want to be besties with a woman who would passively watch you be demeaned or attacked without offering assistance?

That doesn't sound like a safe situation, emotionally or physically. Well, that is exactly what a Phony will do. She'll be your hype man pumping you up; hell, she might even take out her own earrings to encourage the development of the fight. But when it comes down to standing with you when you need her, she will be nowhere to be found, only to magically appear afterward, "worried" about your well-being. If she is only marginally invested in your friendship, that small quota of concern does not translate to her potentially getting a black eye, broken nail, or a sore throat from yelling in your defense.

She is the same when it comes to interacting with people who may not like you. Our friends can have other friendships. It is juvenile to believe that our friendship has the right to constrict her interactions with other women. However, these interactions should never include any kind of conversation about you, regardless of the content. If you have a friend who is friends with someone who openly berates you and she says nothing about it, or worse, contributes to that conversation, she is a Phony. Because her friendship with you is only important when it benefits her.

The Tale of Two Friendships

Kiesha and Nia had bad blood. After too long a span of time, Kiesha made the smart decision to disengage from their relationship. Kiesha's friend Jayda was not involved in that friendship or its demise. She continued her own, separate, friendship with Nia. Other mutual friends informed Kiesha that Jayda often allowed Nia to say negative things about her without any rebuttal. Kiesha kept the information in the back of her mind but never acted on it.

Jayda sometimes volunteered information about state of her friendship with Nia, despite Kiesha never asking. Jayda told her of multiple occasions Nia has asked about her or was jealous of their relationship. Considering Kiesha was deliberate in never asking about Nia or initiating a conversation that could potentially lead to discussing her, she wondered how she was still present in their friendship. The repeat conversations that were had about her between Jayda and Nia started to disturb her. If their lives had no intersection other than Jayda, there was no reason she should be included in their conversations.

When the relationship between Kiesha and Jayda abruptly ended, Jayda got even closer to Nia. Kiesha never spoke ill of Nia, so there was no petty gossip for Jayda to relay. However, she was uncomfortable with the information her former friend, Jayda, had about her own personal life. Do they still talk about her? Have they discussed intimate details that she shared with Jayda in confidence?

That is the unsettling feeling a Phony will leave you with: uncertainty. If our friends are friends with people we are not fond of, it only works if they are able to completely isolate those relationships. In this case, Jayda regularly struggled throughout their friendship to keep her association with Kiesha and Nia separate. Because of that gray area, Kiesha now feels exposed and her privacy unprotected.

A Phony is deceptive because she can possess so many toxic traits in one. For example, she could easily be incorrectly defined as a Male Enthusiast, should she have a sordid tryst with your man behind your back. Unknowingly to you, she only became your friend to try to steal your significant other from you in the first place. She wasn't being sympathetic when she was so attentively listening to you vent. She was gathering precious Intel about the problems you were going through, buying her time, and waiting to use this information in her pursuit of your place. Instead of recognizing she was never truly your friend to begin with, you will just see her surface actions as her toxicity. As a result, you'll add her actions to the list of examples of why you can't trust women around your man.

The problem with that is, she was never your friend, but you didn't know that. Now she has an effect on how you view and approach your future friendships. She does not have a split personality, possessing two completely different and conflicting personality traits. She is two-faced; meaning, she is intentionally showing you a specific side of herself, and hiding the more harmful side to serve a secret agenda.

How to Deal with Phonies

Unfortunately for us, it can be difficult to discern the real from the fake until we are in a position in which support is needed but not found. She is an actress, convincingly playing the role until her needs are met or she gets bored with the performance. Depending on the caliber of her skills, we can easily be mesmerized by her talent of deception. For most of the toxic traits, I advise to work on it in some capacity. I say give her chance to grow past it. I say determine the level of toxicity before writing her off and deciding she is un-friendable. When it comes to a Phony, I say, "Bye, Felicia."

A Phony is like a mirage. She is an oasis promising to quench your thirst in the friendship desert. You'll end up dying from dehydration waiting for that delusion to be something real. It takes enough energy to sustain a legitimate friendship, without wasting our time on a friendship with someone who isn't even honest about being present. If you are fortunate enough to see a Phony for exactly what she is, do not question whether you are being selfish by walking away. You were probably the only person involved in the friendship in the first place.

Dear Phonies,

Since you like to pretend so much, let me act like I care about you becoming a better person. I don't really. I think you are a lost cause, but just in case there is anything of substance underneath all those trifling actions, I will give it an honest try.

You make women insecure and confused. You make them question themselves and other women who have good intentions. You are the reason women have hearts filled with hesitations and memories that shadow their future. There will be many women who read these different traits and feel like they can deal with the people in their lives that embody them. But when they get to you, when they read about you, they will throw their hands up in despair and they will shake their heads in disbelief because they will remember what you did to them. They will see what you are doing to them. They will realize there are no redeeming qualities to be found in someone who never wanted to be anything but a friend to themselves. Is that your goal? Do you want to be that woman? Do you really want to be seen that way?

If you answered yes to any of the above, I hope that your trickster ways and your sketchy motivations find you alone on a deserted island with the ghosts of your friendship past haunting you. Your fraudulent behavior is the biggest danger to women who just want to enjoy the presence of one another. Please do not participate in any relationship until you appreciate its purpose. Hint: in case the message is still lost, your happiness is not the *sole* purpose.

THE OPPORTUNIST

Toxic Tip: All money ain't good money.

Her Toxic Scale: "Can I borrow a dollar?" to "Can you co-sign for my apartment?"

Let's give it up for the woman who knows about every deal on Groupon. The one who has the inside connection to the hottest clubs. Round of applause for the woman who has somehow gotten the lecture notes for free. We love her. We need her. If she weren't around, life would be a lot more... ordinary and expensive. She is always in upward motion. She knows all the right people, at the right times, and is constantly putting herself in the right situation. You as her friend and right-hand woman get to share in the glory of her good fortune.

This is the Opportunist of our dreams: the woman who can get it all and doesn't mind sharing some with you. Seeking better for yourself or wanting friends that are eager to keep moving up the ladder is not a negative thing. The problem is, this isn't always the Opportunist we get. Sometimes we get the friend who can't see their chance to get ahead means we end up getting used.

She doesn't just get the best concert tickets. She gets the best concert tickets from you, with your employee discount, but doesn't invite you to enjoy the concert with her. Then she manages to forget you exist until you see her at will call. Eventually, you magically cross her mind to hang out. Yay, right? She manages to reel you back in with just enough attention to keep you around until, you guessed it, she can ask for more tickets. That is when a good thing for someone else can turn into a bad thing for you. Being the hook-up is one thing; being treated like you're only the hook-up is another. There are sacrifices we are all willing to make for the ones we love; however, an Opportunist operates to the point that exchange becomes so one-sided, it is toxic.

Too Good for My Own Good

Asia has a knack for giving the most to the most undeserving. Her life has been seemingly defined by having the same toxic, parasitic relationship over and over with the same type of woman with different names. She would never consider herself braggadocios, but she would often lead with what she could add to their lives to prove to them that she was a good investment. Not everyone used this against her, but for the Opportunists, it was like a neon sign labeling her as the perfect person to exploit.

Many times in relationships, instead of being seen and treated as a person, Asia's friendship was viewed as a commodity. She could assist writing this paper, she could contribute that money, she could make those decorations, and she could organize these events, all for her friends. Her desire to be a good friend that goes above and beyond for her friends seemed to attract people whose principal interest was in capitalizing on her good will. Too many friends wanted Asia to be convenient, but she was human. She felt like prey and could not restrict herself enough to protect herself from the women who knew she would upgrade them. She saw the patterns and signs. She could foresee the impending issue. Neither ability stopped her from believing that this time would be different.

The Opportunist requires you to maintain the friendship by continuing to give to them, do for them, promote them, build them, and focus primarily on them. They offer friendship with a contingency plan. If you are not constantly enhancing their lives, they will move on to another person, another opportunity, to get their ceaseless needs met.

The difference between an Opportunist and a Phony is that an Opportunist can genuinely like you and want to be your friend. You will just never trump their quest to gain. You and your relationship will be sacrificed the moment something better appears on the horizon. It will never matter how much you have done for an Opportunist in the past. They are the walking, talking, and breathing representation of the song "What have you done for me lately?" Your current deed is only a temporary appeasement until your next one.

The Bottom Feeder

The Bottom Feeder is the Opportunist's happy, lowly sister. They have the same DNA with slightly different outcomes. How can someone who is the lowest on the totem pole be part of the Opportunist Family? Seeking anything seems like an exact contrast of personality to someone who is content on living on the bottom rungs of life. Don't be fooled.

Have you never met someone who has no income but still manages to be at the same places, buying the same things you are? Have you ever lent someone money in an emergency, only to see them magically have money for something frivolous shortly after? How about the person who can live rent or bill free because of their lack of income, who never discusses ways they plan to improve their situation? They are content with allowing someone else having the responsibility of providing for them and living off the hard work of others.

Cousin, Could You Please?

Mal tries to support her family as much as possible. She believes in lifting while she climbs. When her cousin Shay struggled to manage her finances, Mal immediately stepped in to supplement where she lacked. To her, that is her place as family and friend. Before Mal knew it, her supplementation was the chief source of her cousin's income. She was no longer helping every now and then; she was bankrolling Shay's lifestyle.

Her cousin regularly contacted her with a sob story about not being able to pay an essential bill. She even had Mal log onto her account to pay it directly to ensure Mal knew she was paying for that specific expense. Then Shay would check into a Las Vegas hotel a day later, as though the two were not correlated. When Mal questioned her about how she could afford to go to on vacation so shortly after she had paid Shay's bill, Shay convinced Mal that her trip was paid for by friends and that she had limited financial responsibilities while on vacation.

Although Shay did not seem entirely truthful, Mal let the situation pass without any additional questions. It is plausible that someone could have paid for her trip, just like she paid for her lights to stay on. Regardless of who paid for what, Mal knew she had more than enough, so she saw it unfair to keep in excess what Shay could use to survive.

That dedication to communal responsibility is what prompted Mal to continue to help. She found herself taking overtime and curtailing her spending. Not because she was saving a down payment for her future home or trying to offset the price of a much-needed vacation. No, Shay needed help with her cable, her children's after-school programs, her portion of the family trip, everything, all the time. She was also getting more comfortable showing that her modest lifestyle was more lavish that she had led Mal to believe. Mal was operating on a strict budget that did not allow for eating out and shopping, while Shay had disposable income to do all those things. So though on paper Mal may have been more well off, Shay was living a more comfortable life.

Shay wasn't interested in progressing beyond the assistance she was getting from Mal. She planned on taking full advantage of her until her well ran dry.

When Mal stopped giving as much to Shay, she predictably noticed a shift in their relationship. She no longer received calls or texts. Gone were the days of cute videos from the kids. All attempts to communicate were initiated by her. If they did speak, there was no interest in discussing Mal's life. Shay was occupied spending a lot of time with a new family member with the disposable income she needed to continue to keep afloat.

That is how the Bottom Feeder takes being an Opportunist to a lower level. They play on their benefactor's sympathy, usually painting a picture of poverty to get all the help they can to stay exactly where they are. They sustain themselves by taking advantage of every opportunity to not be any more productive than necessary. Their only efforts are spent on capitalizing on other women's efforts. These aren't the women who have fallen on hard times and are relying on your kindness to get them over the hump. There is absolutely nothing wrong with needing help in life. These are the women who see their slump as a chance to take an infinite vacation from responsibility. Moseying through life doing the bare minimum and getting the maximum from other people.

How to Deal with Opportunists

Don't get pimped by your pals. That is a simple, comical, and somewhat sad way of remembering a serious lesson. Do not let someone place a value on your friendship based on the quantity of things you can do for them. If you do, you aren't their friend; you're their sponsor. There is a huge difference between buying your friend's new book (wink wink), and being responsible for paying her rent while she writes it. We should invest in the things that make our friends happy, like promoting their open mic night. We should be considerate of their finances, like picking up the tip when you select a restaurant above their price point. Those considerations should never extend to financing your friendship. Not with your connections, not with your time, and never with your money.

If you get the gut feeling that you are being utilized more than you are being appreciated, stop providing whatever service that is making you feel that way. If at that point your friend begins to distance herself or directly question your dedication to the friendship without that contribution, you are being played. The only way to turn the tables on an Opportunist is by removing their chance to come up. Now, if your friend is gracious and thankful for all that you have done and remains as connected to you once there is nothing to be gained, you know that they simply needed your help. You can choose from that point whether you want to amp up the support or keep it at a level where you never have question her motives. Either way, you will know for certain whether you have a friend that is loyal to you or the hustle of you.

Dear Opportunists,

I hope you don't purposely overstep this critical boundary of friendship. Therefore, I will address you as though you are not intentionally mistreating the people whom you should be thanking. I am going to act as though you have so much drive that sometimes you don't see yourself running over other people. I can for a moment consider that you are ignorant about coming off as someone who is only in the friendship for what they can get from it. That allowance from me, and the women you deal with, is temporary.

If you have recognized any of the Opportunist attributes in yourself, and you shrugged off that deep-down feeling that you have been pretty crummy, then you no longer get that benefit of doubt. You are now fully aware that you hold your friendship for ransom, and instead of rectifying that, you're convincing yourself that you are so amazing you warrant that price. You are greatly overestimating your worth. Someone who cannot have friends without demanding a specific outcome is a depreciating asset.

See, as life progresses, two things happen. We recognize how little it takes to be happy, and we realize we have a lot less to give to try to make people happy. What we retain between those two is the ability to live, to laugh, and to love. These aren't things that can be traded and upgraded. These things are exchanged and elevated between spirits. Seeing as your soul is only for sale to the highest bidder, chances are you'll miss this revelation because you're too accustomed to the game of capitalization.

Don't you worry your pretty little head. I promise should you find yourself older and alone, with a lot of great possessions acquired through never letting a friendship stand in the way of your success, you may meet a younger version of your former self. She will be wrapped in karma, hungry, and anxious to stand on the heads of other women to reach for the stars. I'm sure she would love to be your friend.

THE OPTIMIST

Toxic Tip: You can't appreciate the silver lining without acknowledging the cloud.

Her Toxic Range: "It'll be okay!" to "It is *always* okay."

Last time I checked, there was nothing wrong with sunshine or rainbows, and good energy was the source of everything beneficial in life. So how in the world could *anyone* that is an Optimist ever be toxic to us? Don't we want someone who can bring light to the darkest corners and raise our spirits out of the depths of despair?

Of course we do.

We want people in our lives who make it better. There are few who can do so better than the friend with the contagious smile and the ability to bring laughter out of the hardest of hearts. She's that rare woman who has not a care in the world. If ever she does stumble while gleefully skipping through life, it never fazes her for more than a moment. How can she do it?

There are not many women with a natural disposition to have an outlook on life that cannot be soured. It is healthy to have peaks, valleys, and plateaus that take you through a range of emotions on any given day. The last thing you want to hear while listening to Christina Aguilera, while balling hysterically and shoving the last bit of a Crunchwrap Supreme in your mouth is, "It's no big deal." Sometimes in an Optimist's attempt to be there for us, they forget to do just that: be there for us.

That is when you experience the rare toxic positivity. There is a difference between "Stop being so negative" and "I understand why you're feeling down about this." We want acknowledgment not dismissal, and support not denial. Their rose-colored glasses don't allow them to empathize with our situation long enough to understand that our glasses are broke and won't be replaced for a week or so.

We need to know that our friends will embrace our moments of weakness as their chance to be the proverbial shoulder, not just the blinding ray of light. We all know life will go on, but do we need to be reminded of that one hour, nineteen minutes, and thirteen seconds after we break up with our beau of the last year?

I Am Really This Happy

Kayla is an Optimist. She wears her Drama-Defending lotion every day and has some extra Sunshine Spray just in case she runs into a swarm of sadness. Even the women who had originally questioned her ability to keep up the optimism have long given up on trying to discredit her popping personality. In fact, many of them became her closest friends. Things were great, just as they should be. Until she met someone new. Then she would have to reprove herself, her life outlook, and her unbreakable spirit all over again.

Every time she met someone who did not have the same outlook, she would have to go through hoops and obstacles before they would accept her completely. Then once again, things were awesome, just as they should be. Until she had a friend with a problem she couldn't smile away. Then she had to figure out how to cope with that negativity without losing herself, or worse, losing her friend by not acknowledging it. Kayla has to constantly ask herself what a healthy amount of negativity to absorb is before it begins to bring her down.

Kayla is an Optimist, but she had to develop a process of receiving and funneling through unpleasant moments and people with the flair for positivity that only she may appreciate. She had to deal with the women of the world, who were unable to accept her as she is. Or accepted her, but then attempted to belittle her or abuse her because they knew it was not in her nature to reciprocate their negativity.

Kayla was not prepared for her happiness to be perceived as a flaw. She still deals with an unfair amount of skepticism. However, she is no longer offended by it. She will defend herself if necessary or console a friend in need, and after that exchange has occurred she will return to her pleasant state of mind. She does not worry about appearing to be "real." She's as real as they come. In her true Optimist fashion, she retains hope that others will see that as well.

Optimists are rare. We should applaud them for being able to survive in a world that was not made for them. Women who can tell the world to go screw itself by smiling at everything thrown at them are the unicorns of the toxic world. Incorrectly seen as weak because they rarely engage in conflict, they are some of the strongest people you can have in your life. Most of them do not stay that way by running to the aid of a friend every time she has an issue. It would be impossible to retain the kind of positivity that a true Optimist has without a bit of avoidance. Going out of the way to avoid drama might seem like a smart thing to do. However, if you become so adept at avoiding conflict that you never develop the skills to address it when it is unavoidable, you are bringing toxicity into your perfect world.

How to Deal with Optimists

Your goal when dealing with Little Miss Sunshine is not to bombard her your version of life. Optimists' happiness doesn't come from not knowing is going on with the world. Happiness is their response. Do not undermine their positivity by assuming they do not have any self-awareness or are detached from reality. They have the same emotions are you; they just deal with them in a unique way. There is a difference between allowing space for them to feel comfortable expressing feelings other than delight and being delighted they are in pain.

It can be difficult to deal with an Optimist because they harness so much positivity that it accentuates the negativity in ourselves. Unconsciously we can find ourselves resenting them or wanting them to fall, just to prove to ourselves that the longevity of their happiness cannot be maintained. Fight that feeling. Again, Optimists are human too. They should not be punished for their ability to stay afloat better than you. If you find yourself intimidated by someone else's happiness, you need to reevaluate why you are being critical of anyone who is rejoicing.

The Optimist's trait doesn't just highlight the best in them, but also the worse in us. It is up to you to reconcile your own deficiency, should you feel you have one. Rather than depend on the Optimist to dim their light to accommodate your darkness, accept them for who they are.

To determine whether your Optimist has a healthy relationship with herself, find out why she committed herself to remaining joyful. Is it her coping mechanism? Was she never allowed to show her emotions as a child? Does she always seek to find the best in every situation? Those questions will reveal whether she is a pure Optimist or just good at hiding her feelings. Caution and observation should be paid to those women who feign happiness but do not truly possess it. Women who smile with tears running down their eyes need someone to ask if they are okay. They need women who will hold their hand even when they are adamant they do not need any assistance. They are the ones who should never have their non-optimistic days thrown in their faces. Quickly judging or dismissing them does not translate to them showing the variance of emotions you want to see.

There are Optimists who lack transparency because they are afraid of losing control over their emotions or of no longer being accepted by those who see them as positive people. That does not mean that they are not authentic; it means they are uncomfortable within themselves or with you. The more you require them to "stop being so damn happy all the time" to prove they are who you want them to be, the more likely you are to ensure you never get to see their entire personality.

Dear Optimists,

I want to thank you. Sincerely. When I was young many people saw me as an Optimist. I was always happy, smiling, and the life of the party. I was also extremely depressed. Most of the time I was lying to myself and the world. It felt good to be happy, even when I knew it wasn't real. Happiness was an addiction for me. I was always chasing the next high point in life, the next laugh, the next moment in the sun. So many people wanted to be around me because I provided a chance for them, momentarily, to be Optimists too.

I admit, I am not a true Optimist at heart. Over time I have shed my faux-glow and have accepted I have too many shadows to ever go back to the bright side. Not naturally. So, when I said you are a true gem to be treasured, I mean it. When people go out their way to criticize and condemn you, recognize that often they are rejecting you because you make them question themselves. Don't let them convince you that you are anything other than the amazing woman you are. Keep spreading your contagious spirit. The world needs you, even if they don't understand you, accept you, want you or appreciate yourself as they should.

If you ever want to frown, I will not be disappointed. It's not that I want you to be unhappy; I want you to know it is okay if you are. You donate so much of your beautiful aura to the world, I imagine occasionally, you feel left empty. But you're not alone. Except when you want to be. Then I totally understand.

Just as I would advise anyone who associates themselves with you to be kind although you are different, I request you do the same. Don't minimize your friends' existences. It can feel as though you are reducing our feelings to small inconveniences instead of full-fledged emotional states. We may very well need you to help us pick ourselves up, but first acknowledge where we are lying. You are the yang to our yin. Hopefully sometimes we'll be your yang instead. But when we need you, it isn't just to smile.

THE PESSIMIST

Toxic Tip: You are a prisoner of your own jail. Pardon yourself.

Her Toxic Scale: "This kind of sucks," to "You suck for trying to be happy."

If you have ever used "Eyore" as a reference to describe a friend, then you know a Pessimist. So obviously jaded by life, this woman has a special ability to bring down a mood, poop out of a party, drag excitement through the mud, and drain the life out of you. We should stop calling them Eyore and just label them vacuums. Dyson vacuums at that. That is how efficient they are at being methodically melancholic.

The opposite of the Optimist, there is no moment bright enough to give them a chance to forget they are doomed. You are doomed for being their friend. Actually, why are you their friend in the first place? They're doomed, remember, so you'll eventually abandon them. You'll have to. *Waaaah waaaah waaaah*. We allow their toxic vortex to suck us in and down into their black abyss, all in the name of friendship. We let the glimmer of hope that shines in us serve as the flicker for them, even when they disappoint us by always being disappointed in themselves. We are stuck forever in a tornado of gloom because she can't muster one reason to cheerful.

Unhappiness 101

Yue was one of the first people Hui met in college. She was a welcome ally in a sea of new faces and places. Hui desperately missed the normalcy of home and wanted their friendship to anchor her to her new surroundings. Transitioning to the rigor of higher education and the cultural changes of a new community can be difficult for even the strongest of people. Hui and Yue were feeling the same strain that most college freshmen do, and they found security in one another.

As the best foot that Yue put forward started to slowly recede and expose the negative nature of her more organic self, Hui did not immediately recognize it as a red flag. Her constantly heavy disposition and input was dismissed as stress and fear. Hui was constantly playing Captain Save a Friend, but nothing could appease Yue. Over time Hui began to think nothing but dismay pleased Yue, when not even the highlights of their friendship was enough to brighten her outlook.

Hui disliked dwelling in the bleak states of mind that Yue created. Although she knew she no longer enjoyed interacting with her, she also lacked the confidence to address it directly. She did not know how to have a conversation about what was upsetting her without creating more conflict, and thus opted for avoidance instead. Looking back, Hui believes they could have retained some aspect of their friendship, had she possessed the maturity and communication skills she does now. As it stands, she is just happy to leave Yue and her pessimism as an undergrad learning experience. She understands some people seek failure the same way some people seek success, and in those circumstances, the best within yourself cannot compensate for the worst within them.

Like every other trait, there is a range of how far and deep the toxic behavior goes. There are Pessimists who focus solely on how they will never reach their full potential. They are clouded in self-doubt and insecurity. Instead of admitting they are struggling within themselves, their personal struggle manifests itself into an outward condemnation of everything else in the world. This is the Pessimist who needs a little TLC. She is misguided in believing she is lacking.

Then there are those women with specific intention. This is the Pessimist who cannot see the good in anything. That is their fatal flaw. Even when things are on the up and up, and everything goes as planned or plays out better than expected, they will still find a reason to bring the thunder, the lightening, the rain, and the complain. This is their unique, and difficult to accept, skill. Beyond her overall sour disposition, her pessimism is not always internal. She also finds ways to undermine your accomplishments. Whether through a little jab about your results or doubt about the probability of your success, she wants to remind you of how poorly it can all turn out. This is when her toxicity turns the page from unnerving to unacceptable.

Friends should critique with care. We should be able to share opinions and ask for advice without questioning the space it comes from. When the Pessimist is involved, you will never know whether you have a great idea or a grand failure. Her input will always stem from a worst-case scenario, leaving you with just enough uneasiness to question the validity of your capabilities. No one needs that type of non-support in their life. The Optimist is looking a little better, isn't she?

Special Note:

I don't want to you to confuse a Pessimist with someone who is clinically or chemically depressed. I am not speaking about those friends who struggle to make it through life because they are trying to manage their illness. I am directly placing the title of toxicity on those who are going through life trying to find fault in every footstep. It is an intentional act for them to fail. Emotional illness can be a precursor to any toxic trait. When deciding if you are dealing with a Pessimist, omit any friends whom you know are actively battling with their mental health. It is unfair and inaccurate to categorize them as Pessimists more than another toxic trait.

You're Making This Hard for Me

Lorrie struggles with depression. It is great that she recognizes the issues she must keep in check in order to be healthy, but this requires constant effort on her end. Not only does she want to feel capable of living the best life she can, she also wants to manage her condition and not burden others with her personal fight. Her efforts make her more compassionate toward others who identify with struggling to do the same. She makes a point to never discount someone else's journey or attempts to mental prosperity because she understands how hard it can be.

Lorrie knows depression looks different on everyone who wears it. However, she began to feel triggered by specific friends who knew her history, lackadaisically using mental health concepts for attention. She felt torn between knowing she needed to focus on fighting for herself and wanting to make sure that she was there for her friends if they also needed assistance.

It was hurtful to realize that those friends who were draining her of the energy required for her own personal upkeep weren't doing so because they were genuinely in an emotional tailspin, but because they knew they could co-opt on her pain. They did not want to work on or change themselves. All they wanted to do was dump their sadness in her lap. It became a dangerous position for Lorrie to be in. She was taking a risk for people who were not actually suffering.

With her open heart and her fragile state, she was susceptible to their negativity. Since she was available, they selfishly gave their pessimism to her without any regard for the outcome. What they needed more than a healthy friend was an open receptacle. They sold their pessimism as equal to her real and difficult life with depression. When she began to limit how much she could absorb, they began to limit how much they associated with her. Their actions verified to Lorrie that she was not a resource, or an extended hand utilized for help, but rather their toxic waste zone to lay out their worst attributes without consequence.

How to Deal with a Pessimist

There is only one way to deal with a Pessimist and stay sane: emotional restriction. You may be unable to distance yourself physically from a college roommate or beloved aunt, but you absolutely do not have to take in everything they release. Restrict yourself from their energy.

We must adapt to utilizing distance as a valuable resource in obtaining our non-toxic life. When it comes to friends or family, we just want to be there. Everything from movies to acclaimed literature tells us we are to remain committed through the good, the bad, and the ugly. We must be white knights, therapists, confidants, and anything else in between. It is a ridiculous pressure that encourages us to stay in relationships that are not healthy.

This is how the Pessimist manages to maintain the friendships they have: irrational pressure and lots of heavy, displaced guilt. The world already hates them. Nothing good ever happens to them. How can you stab them in the back and deal the final blow by ending the friendship? While you can never change her perspective, sometimes she does need to be loved a little harder, praised a little stronger and assisted a little more. However, you should never do any of these things to the point of exhaustion. Just try to understand that her pessimism may not be genuine. It can be a defense mechanism masquerading as her personality, just like with the Optimist. The more she finds pleasure in the person she is, the less likely she will perpetrate the worst aspects of this trait.

Pessimists can get so distracted in finding ways to sabotage themselves that they lose track of how they have already hindered their relationships. Bring it to their attention. Let them learn direct results of their negative behavior and cross your fingers that they are encouraged them to modify it. Example: If you have a friend who always complains about the service you will receive at a restaurant before you even sit down, stop going out to eat with her. Should she question why you guys no longer dine together, politely and directly tell her she seems to not enjoy the experience. There is a chance she is unaware of how much she is killing your vibe.

Dear Pessimist,

You're the kind of woman who makes other women scrunch up their faces in confusion while asking, "Who hurt you?" We want to know how, out of all the paths you could have taken, you managed to walk down the only one with cracked soil, dead foliage, and no light at the end. Your existence seems to be composed of nothing but gray matter. How did you get here? Or better yet, why did you stay?

As much as we want to try to make sense of why you are the way you are, it would be even better if you would try too. How you approach life isn't healthy. Therefore, being around you, being your friend, loving you, becomes unhealthy for us as well. It would be so dope if you acknowledged there is more to life than the clouds and rain, or at least that those things are the only way rainbows can happen.

Whatever is holding you back from happiness is deeper than demonstrating how life's ups and downs work. It's deeper than explaining cause and effect. Only you can moderate your internal voice that tells you, "This too is a parade to downpour on." Only you can determine how to rationalize those irrational thoughts. Only you can turn that frown upside down. I hope you do what no one else can do for you, or you will be someone no one else can be around.

THE COMPETITOR

Toxic Tip: Seek out people who bring out the best in you more than they want to be better than you.

Her Toxic Scale: "What did you get on the final?" to "Let's compare tax returns."

You are on the elliptical machine literally trying to sweat your ass off, pushing toward your personal best. And when those final seconds wind down, you enact a small parade in your own honor because you *totally* just owned that workout!

You and your bestie are determined to get bikini ready by Memorial Day weekend if it's the last thing you do. She is at the gym every time you are, usually already warming up before you get there. She volunteers to meal prep with you every week, often comparing her macros to yours. She is so supportive, right? Or is she? Does she do so well with dieting and exercise because she is extremely focused, or because she refuses to be outdone by you? Competition is a natural. But we face enough challenges throughout our day without having to wonder whether the person gliding next to us is watching our machine only to make sure they are doing just a little bit more.

Even if it is not the most worrisome toxic trait, it is the most annoying. How can you celebrate killing a hundred crunches if you know there will just be a "Well I did one hundred and one" moment right after? So, don't work out with her. Problem solved, right? Until the next phone she has to get before you, the better sandwich she has to make, the more attractive man she has to find, or the better credit score she has to have. Enough!

These women are unable to set their own standard of achievement, so they determine that their bar of success is just a notch above yours. You can't even have a bad day without her comparing her entire life of hardship to yours. We want friends, not rivals. When the ones close to us see their next conquest instead of their next great conversation, the connection can become more battleship than friendship.

I Do... Not

Meagan was a bridesmaid in Lisa's wedding. She thought her wedding was nice and fit the couple's personalities well. She would have done a few things differently, but that is the cool thing about weddings, you just do what works for you. When Meagan got engaged she was excited to offer Lisa the opportunity to stand by her at the altar. Lisa happily accepted. Before Meagan could even begin to discuss her color choices or venue options, she felt Lisa trying to control her nuptials. She critiqued every decision made, but also magically forget the information for her florist that Meagan had requested. Meagan started to feel like Lisa didn't want to help her have the best wedding but instead to plan her exact wedding again, only not as nice.

When Meagan stopped reaching out to her for advice or assistance, Lisa grew angry and combative. She questioned her motivation for secrecy and began venting her frustration to the other bridesmaids.

Lisa even signed up for major components of Meagan's bridal shower but dropped the ball at the last minute, leaving the other bridesmaids to scramble to give Meagan a great shower.

Miraculously, they were able to get down the aisle and through the night without any major disturbances. Or so Meagan thought. Some weeks after the wedding, some of the other guests and bridesmaids filled Meagan in on Lisa's antics that night. Between Lisa's inebriation and belief that Meagan went out of her way to outdo her wedding, she decided the best use of her night was telling anyone who'd listen how terrible the wedding was. From the ceremony to last call, nothing Meagan did was right, and Lisa was sure to point it out.

After being updated on Lisa's shenanigans, Meagan was less than pleased with her friend. She couldn't figure out how a day that was supposed to be for her and her husband focused so much on Lisa. They did not speak again for close to a year. It was only after seeing one another at a friend's event did they meet with level heads and hash things out. There was a much-needed apology from Lisa and very gracious forgiveness from Meagan. They remain on speaking terms, but Meagan doesn't plan to invite Lisa to any additional life events. Not even a birthday party.

A Competitor cannot cheer themselves on and cheer you on at the same time, so they can never be genuinely enthused for you. Even Non-Competitors have the nonsensical mentality that we should first size people up to decide if they are a threat to us emotionally, financially, or physically. After our initial assessment, we then choose how we will deal with them. Typically, Competitors only fully embrace women once they determine they are not a threat to them in any capacity. Those that present as a danger to their ego are generally either treated with restraint or as contenders. It is ridiculous to only want to be associated with women you are confident you outshine. Is it ever even a competition if you only pick opponents that fit comfortably within your insecurities?

That's what makes friending a Competitor so toxic; you can never win. Literally if you win, it's a problem for her. If you never win, it is a problem for you. We all occupy our own lanes. When they cross or exist on the same road, you should still drive like you're the only one on that street. Competitors spend so much time looking in front of them, around them, and behind them, they can't comprehend their own GPS should be propelling them forward.

The Hater: The Useless Competitor

I want to shout out to all my Haters! All the women who went out of their way to try to bring me down, say something negative about me, or just hate for the sake of hating. But, would one of my haters even be reading my book? I wouldn't spend a copper coin to promote the dream of someone I didn't like, but I'm not a Hater. Unfortunately, they can reside a little closer to home. The green-eyed monster can transform anyone, given the right circumstances. It's not just the woman who openly despises you; it is also the woman who likes you but can't stand that you are achieving at a pace that makes her uneasy. That promotion you have been waiting on, that thesis you just completed, or that home you just purchased can become a point of contention and a source of pain for someone else merely by happening.

Do they hate you? Probably not. But that doesn't mean they can't hate that you have something they do not have, *even* if they don't want it for themselves. A Hater isn't always controlled by specifics, which can be confusing. If they don't want it or haven't worked for it, why does it matter if we have it? Because, jealousy. Because, inadequacy. Because, insecurity. Because, instability. Because... hate. If someone is not one hundred percent invested in their own joy, can they give you one hundred percent when it's your moment to shine? A Hater decides that your happiness directly impacts the amount of happiness available for them.

More Than Poppin'

Lynn posted a picture of herself on social media. Shortly after, amongst the other comments, she was given a compliment on the awesomeness of her eyebrows. That's no big deal, just an acknowledgment of a small aspect of her overall attractiveness. She made a point to let her esthetician know she was recognized for her efforts. What did a Hater, Erinn, do? She soon commented to discredit that small compliment by saying, "I hope that people are not only recognizing your eyebrows as your beauty." For no real reason, she interrupted Lynn's moment of arched glory to negate the value of someone else's appreciation.

Why would Erinn feel the need to do this? Is it because she didn't think of it first? Did she wish it were said to her instead? Did she only want to define Lynn by her own standards? Lynn didn't know. None of these reasons explain why someone else telling Lynn that her esthetician is skilled was too much for her to handle. She wanted Lynn to believe that she undeserving of a compliment, as though that is a compliment itself.

Erinn wasn't upset about ever-changing beauty expectations or the obsession with standardizing appearances within the media. Those are legit concerns that could warrant a social critique. She wasn't concerned about Lynn's wellbeing or her self-esteem. She could not handle Lynn's shine being brighter than her own appearance or opinion, even if it was just Lynn's eyebrows.

A Hater is different from a Pessimist. A Hater is only a downer when it comes to you being uplifted. Instead of admitting that you exude or possess something they find desirable, they attempt to dismantle your character or accomplishments. Saying you're "too big for your britches" sounds much better than, "I'm upset that you're winning for no valid reason."

A Hater is rarely ever in your league, even if they are in your life as an active participant. I don't mean "in your league" as in they are not as intelligent, attractive, or important. They are not in your league because they have stopped seeing you as a person and only view you as a concept. Not even a bar to rise to or a goal to match. You are now just something to dislike because they feel like disliking. This woman is not in your league. Don't entertain her eye-rolling, teeth-sucking, passive aggressive comments or her not-so-subtle tendency to speak negatively of you to others. She doesn't deserve the satisfaction.

How to Deal with Competitors

Once you figure out you are dealing with a Competitor, you have a decision to make. You can compete, or you can thrive. Don't play the game. Choose to thrive. When we have a friend who has competitive tendencies, sometimes to keep her at peace within herself, we lessen our success. We do this either because we don't want to make her feel bad or because we don't want to deal with her constantly trying to outdo us. Both cater to her comfort. What about you? Should you not be able to exist within your friendship without the condition that you stay beside or one foot behind her? Competitors want a continuous baseline or marker for reference. Be so uniquely yourself, she has no choice but to realize competing with you is impossible because you are different people.

This can be difficult if the relationship is in a less personal setting. If it is within the workplace or an organization where you are looking to advance up the ladder, show up and show out. Competition within business is necessary and to be expected. A true competitor, not a toxic one, will respect your grind as she masters hers. Once that desire to be compared and outdone leaves the field, court, boardroom, or cohort, you are entering the toxic zone and you need to reevaluate the purpose of the relationship. Anyone who can only value you to a level they set is not someone you need to share your life with.

Dear Competitors,

Say this every morning as your new mantra: "The only person I am competing against is who I was yesterday." Say it until you memorize it. Say it until it begins to ring true.

Girl, having a relationship with you can be a real drag. You may not drain us like the Pessimist, but you are just a tiresome. The constant counting of stats is weighing your friendship down. Set us both free by waving the checkered flag and declaring this the last lap.

You think you need to be the best person in the room. Do tell me, what happens when you leave that room? What happens when you leave that building, campus, or city? There will be women who are stronger or smarter. You will meet women who have hustled harder or are just more interesting. Who cares? You should be focused on being the best version of yourself.

If you spent as much time lifting yourself up as you do ensuring everyone else is down, you would be better off. Qualifying your own happiness through the success, or lack thereof, of others is counterintuitive in the long run. Find women who make you laugh and not ones who make you feel superior. Find women who challenge you and motivate you in a positive way. Competition isn't the problem; you are. Making it the basis of your self-worth and relationships is toxic. Shine not because you believe everyone to be dull, but because you know even in this large universe, you're still one fabulous star.

THE PERSUADER

Toxic Tip: You don't always have to give an opinion.

Her Toxic Range: "Let's run a 5k!" to "Let's join a cult!"

There are those who lead and those who follow. There are women who naturally draw crowds without effort. Their ideas and feelings manage to garner more attention than most others around them. Organically able to provide direction and wisdom, they can make even ordinary things appear more alluring. These women stand so firmly in their beliefs that you begin to believe them as well. This is the kind of Persuader that can change the world, in a good way. When given a platform and a meaningful message, their energy can move communities forward. Their drive can make the difference between where we are and where we want to be.

Then there are Persuaders, who believe they are this person, when, in actuality, they would be better off doing more listening than talking. They have the same natural skill of persuasion, but it is used for personal benefit and gain instead of consideration for the people they are influencing. Often weaker than they pretend to be, they are secure only in their opinion, or in the opinions that can best serve them. That is why they scream them so loudly over all others.

Which makes you wonder, is she pushing you to wear that barely there dress because she really believes it is the best outfit for you, or because she doesn't want to be the only one with the increased probability of a wardrobe malfunction? Does she really want to experience going to France with you? Or is she just trying to split the costs with someone else and you seem like the perfect person to help her foot the bill? The toxic dilemma of the Persuader is knowing when the encouragement is going too far. Are they trying to bring out the best in you or convinced they know best for you?

No Eat, Pray, or Love

Kyrsten's best friend JoJo has recently reestablished her relationship with her church. She goes to Sunday worship, Tuesday Bible study, and Friday choir rehearsal. It is difficult for Kyrsten to accept that JoJo is spending so much time at church. Initially, Kyrsten assumed it was because the Fridays JoJo now spent at church used to be the ones they spent at Happy Hour, and it sucked to lose her go out pal. But, it wasn't just the drinks shared that was being lost; it was also their time together. Kyrsten understood that JoJo's priorities had shifted, but it didn't take away the sting of no longer being one of her priorities. She had to adjust.

Being cognizant of JoJo's new life path, Kyrsten asked JoJo to spend time with her when JoJo was not otherwise busy at church. Even requests for a lunch date were refused and replaced with an offer to go to service instead. Considering that she wasn't asking for JoJo to miss Sunday worship to have Sunday brunch, Kyrsten couldn't quite understand why JoJo couldn't eat out on a Saturday—or why she believed bringing Kyrsten to church would serve as an adequate substitute. When Kyrsten asked JoJo to accompany her to the movies, again JoJo redirected her request with an offer to attend a church event instead.

At this point Kyrsten was growing frustrated with JoJo. She felt slighted because she made sure JoJo knew she was taking her dedication seriously, and JoJo would not give her the same consideration. She was practically demanding that she accompany her on this spiritual journey in order to spend time with her.

Kyrsten decided to stop trying, but that did not prevent JoJo from continuously bombarding her with offers to attend church events. Unwilling to be the only one to compromise, she requested that JoJo no longer reach out to her solely to bring her into her church-fold. She knew where to find them.

She could understand JoJo not wanting to participate in various activities that did not suit her current lifestyle. However, she thought eating and laughing were still things that they could share without either battling her morals. Unfortunately, JoJo felt otherwise.

A year later, JoJo still attends church regularly but has found herself loosening the self-imposed restrictions on herself and the people around her. She contacted Kyrsten hoping they could hang out over dinner. Kyrsten refused. It was never about why JoJo alienated herself, or that she decided to change her life. It was the way she decided that Kyrsten could only exist in it within the capacity that best fit for her. For Kyrsten, JoJo's need to be obeyed was a deal-breaker. She remained cordial, but they were never close again.

Everything that a Persuader encourages us to do isn't negative. However, it may not be for us. Their heart can be in the right place, even if their actions seem a little off-putting. I know many friends who have beautiful religious relationships and want the world to know. That is awesome. But does that mean we need to go to every church retreat to prove our dedication to them? Absolutely not. It is unfair for anyone to impose their ideals on us. We love friends who are eager to upgrade us, but if their attempt at persuasion has made them comfortable with being our authority and executioner, then we need to set some boundaries.

When the Persuader dismisses your feelings as insignificant because it does not align with what they want to do or see you do, a toxic environment will develop. You deserve to be an equal partner in your friendship. Once you voice what you are willing to do, based off your schedule, morals, health, or anything else, your friend should listen and receive that information. I specify between hearing and understanding because sometimes there is a disconnect between those two actions. A Persuader it is not always ignorant of your feelings, but their own feelings make them unable to internalize it. If you are aware you are a strong personality, or that you are dealing with one, keeping communication open means listening as much as you speak.

Older Ain't Wiser

Tabitha has an older cousin, Debra, who lives with her. Within their family, age hierarchy plays a large role in how everyone is expected to act toward one another. Therefore, Tabitha found herself on the lower end of the totem pole of respect because of her birth year. She was constantly playing politics with her emotions because she was never free to express herself and have those thoughts appreciated. Her cousin took advantage of her position within the family by both persuading Tabitha to do as she instructed and convincing Tabitha's mother that she deserved to have a certain amount of control over Tabitha. She wanted her opinions and directions to be adhered to without hesitation. Debra felt powerful and enjoyed the adoration, however forced.

Tabitha's mother saw Debra as the perfect person to guide Tabitha through a host of adolescent issues in a less maternal and more relatable way. Had her mother bothered to ask Tabitha directly what she needed, Tabitha would have gladly explained to her how she was being mistreated and conned.

As Tabitha matured, she realized much of what Debra told her was either false or irrelevant. She wanted to continue to keep the peace amongst everyone in the family; however, she began to ignore Debra's advice. Debra was further removed from the life that Tabitha was living than she willing to accept. Tabitha needed to make her own choices based off her feelings.

Instead of embracing a change in the relationship and respecting Tabitha's ability to make sound decisions on her own, Debra continued to try to persuade her to do things the way she instructed. Whenever Tabitha refused, Debra would complain to Tabitha's mother. Instead of being a loving confidant, Debra ended up being a mini-dictator, insistent that she knew enough to make final decisions. What hurt Tabitha the most is that instead of having an amazing relationship with a super cool cousin, she ended up resenting and avoiding Debra.

A subsidiary persona of the Persuader is the know-it-all. She knows it all, has seen it all and can tell you all... always. They're so impressed with themselves, and they're convinced at the sheer volume of knowledge they have, that they believe you should follow them blindly. But, you don't need your friends to have the instructions for your life. You have your mother for that, and she is already enough. The Persuader can't grow within the friendship if she believes she has nothing to learn from you. If she thinks your own thoughts about your life are inadequate, do you have a friend, or an adviser?

How to Deal with a Persuader

When anyone is pushing you towards any idea that is not your own, you must immediately question why. Do not stop asking yourself that question until you feel comfortable with the answer. Admittedly, I am not completely unbiased when it comes to this trait. But that does not prevent me from being just as critical. With less toxic Persuaders, they are likely unaware when their opinions dominate a friendship. My, I mean their, intent does not make up for the fact that you can feel silenced or unrecognized. Regardless of their position on the toxic scale, with a Persuader, you will have to speak up and demand their attention. If they want someone to do as they are told, they need a puppy, not a friend. You are your own individual. If you are persuaded to do anything, by anyone, it should be your most awesome self. Keep repeating that fact for yourself and for them as needed.

Also remember, a Persuader cannot get you to do anything without your permission. Don't give consent to someone else to lead you. Every action you take, regardless of the motivation, is your choice. No, you do not have to go back to spin class after you felt the discomfort of sitting on that death seat and vowed to never again subject your butt to that wide plastic thong. Not if it's your friend's favorite workout, not if that's how she lost fifty pounds, and not if she is the instructor. Go to body pump class and don't feel bad about it. Everything is not for everyone; real friends understand that.

No relationship can be dependent on one person participating in the other's preferred interest and remain healthy. Travel through life with people who understand there are multiple routes they did not think of toward happiness.

Dear Persuaders,

Simmer down sometimes and learn to put yourself on timeout. I get it. You are trying to save the world one person at a time. Try not to forget you are dealing with women, not clones and not robots. Your actions, especially if you find yourself frequently encouraging others, have consequences. Unless your goal is to take responsibility for all those whom you intentionally influence, you may want to think about whom you are persuading and what you are endorsing.

Relationships can be modified to respect even the most polarizing life paths. The way that happens is by respecting the other woman's decisions in life and not trying to persuade her to act according to your lifestyle. If you have a friend who strictly adheres to the Catholic doctrine, do not try to convince her to go out for drinks. That shows disrespect to her faith and her position in your friendship. Just as if a friend has recently undergone weight loss surgery and is focusing on her food intake, it would be rude to offer an all-you-can-eat buffet as a restaurant option. Don't try to convince her "one more bite won't hurt," because it could.

This advice also goes directly to the people who persuade for a living. Influence is not a right; it is a responsibility. If you are a in a position of power with the ability to make a difference, do so wisely. Whether you are a politician, blogger, critic, or celebrity, you are still responsible for the energy, the words, and the products you choose to elevate. If money is your only motivation and you're using it to persuade women to buy things that will not actually improve their quality of life, you're failing. If you are persuading them to do things that only improve your life, you are doing it wrong.

Life is about value. You're either increasing or decreasing the value of someone's life with every opinion you give. Carry that burden. Feel that weight. If it makes you uncomfortable, stop jumping to the front of the line to lead. If you find yourself always at the front of the line, stand back every now and then and see if you are doing so to the detriment of those behind you. You might be blocking the path and holding people back more than you are propelling them forward. Operate with a purpose beyond yourself if you lead a community. Serve and give service. And lastly, give others a chance to seek themselves, by themselves for themselves.

THE PACK

Toxic Tip: If you need a squad with you to go to battle, you're not ready for war.

Her Toxic Range: "Pink Ladies" to "Mean Girls"

This is commonly the first toxic relationship we encounter. My first interaction with this unique beast was in grade school. Every year since then, I have either been part of a Pack or attacked by one, and often experienced both at the same time. That is the most disheartening aspect of it of this trait: we become Pack oriented so early. First as a source of safety and comfort. Then that innocent concept of camaraderie begins to include elements of judgment and separation, and that quickly sullies a good thing.

What makes the Pack toxic? The communal decision-making that instantly restricts individual thought and reaction. There is a reason you always hear someone proclaim mob mentality as a factor of their poor decision-making. The key factor in distinguishing the toxicity of a Pack is determining if the women within that group would treat you the same if you were separate from the members. If their individual toxicity is the result of feeling either comfort or intimidation by the Pack around them, that is a problem. Otherwise, you just have a group of women who all happen to just not like you. That sucks, but it isn't toxic.

There is nothing that brings people together more than a common enemy. Having the space to identify, critique, and condemn someone as a group leaves little time to do the same to those in our inner circle. The result is, "We within the pack are the same, they outside of it are different, and because of that, we don't accept them." We learn this so young that by the time we reach adulthood, we are in a cycle of leaving and joining different Packs as a norm. We begin to define ourselves by our Pack accomplishments and label others by their Pack tendencies. Unified by the fear of being outside of the "in crowd," women can do some hateful things to show "loyalty" to their own. The sweet girl you grew up with can turn into the spiteful spawn of the devil himself, depending on who is sitting at her lunch table. Think about how strong the desire to be included within the Pack must be to make dysfunction feel necessary.

What Happens in Vegas, Stays in Vegas

Well, if you ruin your friendship in Sin City, chances are it will still be ruined once you return home. LeShawn went to Vegas with a group of friends. They had traveled together before; therefore, she didn't anticipate anything other than continued good times. Quickly one of her friends, Miko, seemed a little off. She wasn't interested in the typical Vegas debauchery; she seemed to want to go full *Hangover*. LeShawn didn't know what was so different about this time. Was the air thinner on the strip? A gambler's high? Sure, there was mass consumption of alcohol, but that was nothing new.

Miko was displaying continuously unsafe behavior and, much to the chagrin of LeShawn, the rest of the group continued dismissing and making excuses for it. She could understand they all wanted to have fun, but watching Miko make bad decisions wasn't fun anymore. There are levels to letting loose. When you're wandering off by yourself, inviting random guys back to the room, and disregarding the safety of the rest of the group, you're not letting loose, you're lost.

LeShawn attempted to sway the group into holding Miko accountable for how she was carrying on. However, for most of the trip, the group was content with accepting and assisting her in continuing her unsafe actions. This caused LeShawn to question not just Miko, but also the group of friends that cosigned what she was doing. Although she considered herself part of the unit, when situations turned dangerous, she bravely made the decision to distance herself from the group and stop enabling Miko. Eventually someone else also spoke out against Miko's actions, which was needed to control the chaos, but it proved to be too little too late. She knew she could never travel with this group again.

The Pack requires participants to fill specific roles. The primary role is the leader. Every pack has a leader, or even a group of leaders, who acts like an executive board of bad decision-making. However, the leaders of the Pack rarely share the responsibility of guiding the direction of the group equally; even the leaders have a leader. The lower leaders are usually granted their position of power by coddling and obeying the main leader. In return for their fealty, they can subjugate others.

Below the leaders there are the eager followers. They are the worker bees of the hive that either believe in the designated agenda or are looking to move up in the Pack. The lowest level of the Pack are those who participate when required and only enough to remain in the good graces of those above them. They are a part of the Pack because they fear being exiled, want the safety of numbers, or wish to remain friends with specific people in the Pack. They do not necessarily believe in or follow the same thought process as everyone else, but they are dues-paying members nonetheless.

All these women don't have to like each other or place high value on their individual friendships. There must be only one important link holding them together that convinces them that associating with one another is more beneficial than remaining separate. For leaders, without their subordinates, there is no one to dominate and to bolster their ego. For those at the bottom, without those above them, there is no one to protect them from other Packs. The bottom needs to get along and top needs to maintain order. The misguided souls in the middle fight for a higher spot or try not to get demoted to the bottom.

Within the Pack itself, there is a constant power play creating tension and an unhealthy dependency. Still, this communal interdependence keeps them together. Not love, not appreciation, not happiness, but fear. This is the toxic Pack. This is the group of women you want to avoid. They are already so unhealthy with one another, having a bad relationship with you is just another notch on their belt. Don't be an accessory. You're better than that.

Sisterhood Struggles

In college, Yvette became interested in joining a sorority. These women were smart, talented, involved in amazing work, and magnetic to be around. Upon initial investigation, her adoration seemed justified. She was amazed and appreciated that she had the opportunity to coexist with so many bomb women. After becoming a member, she enjoyed all the benefits of being in the organization. The warmth of sisterhood and the support of like-minded peers was everything she had hoped for when pursuing initiation.

She would've never guessed that the bonds she believed she was forging within the organization would be weakened and eventually severed the moment she did not agree with some aspects of the chapter's traditions. Participating in any organization requires a certain amount of compromise and consideration. Yvette could accept that. What she couldn't accept is that there was never any room for her own voice to be heard amongst the senior members.

When she confided in the sisters she was closest to about her concerns, they often supported her privately, then joined the ranks in unison publicly. They never wanted to risk disturbing the safety of their lowly position. The number of people within the organization she felt she could trust to act as individuals reduced. She began avoiding interactions with the people who proudly followed along and those on the fringes who were silently accepting.

The idea of unity and blind allegiance appeared synonymous for those in the group and completely toxic to Yvette. She joined the organization to sing in a chorus, not to set up the microphones for the same soloists.

Despite Yvette's desire to be involved with many of the individuals in the group, she found herself only associating with those who had also distanced themselves from the stifling politics of the organization. She just couldn't associate with people who were selective with being themselves. Their relationship was based on mutual respect and not required submission; therefore, Yvette didn't feel like she was in a toxic situation anymore and got to experience the sisterhood she initially sought, just on a smaller scale.

All group dynamics aren't unhealthy. However, the moment you start to wonder whether your presence is less important than your adherence, you may want to determine if being a piece of the puzzle is better than being your own work of art. If you are consistently sacrificing your values in order to be a member of a specific group, you're hanging with the wrong people. Friendships, even those based on similarities, should allow for differences to not just be tolerated, but appreciated.

How to Deal with the Pack

Every group of friends isn't a gang attacking all who have not been initiated into their intimate fold. However, enough unhealthy Packs exist to make everyday life unbearable at times. The Pack at work, the Pack at school, the Pack at home... these are groups of women we encounter constantly. The attack on the Pack is about prevention and protection: preventing yourself from being active in a pack that can bring toxicity to others and protecting yourself from the packs that want to pass their toxicity onto you.

From the Inside:

The Pack depends on the unified actions of its members. If everyone agrees to do the same thing, that will be the outward action that is displayed. If you participated, you are responsible for that group action. Do not use peer pressure as an excuse for yourself. You made an individual decision, and it was still your choice.

Keep that in mind when offered the opportunity to act as a group. No matter what, you'll be held responsible as your own woman. A group trip to NYC sounds like a great idea. A group trip to slash your bestie's ex's new girlfriend's tires sounds like property damage. It sounds like a mug shot. If you are on the soccer team and the idea of making an offensive poster comes up, whether you are buying the supplies, designing the layout, or never objecting, you are willfully participating. Continuously check yourself and your motives to ensure that you remain the person you want to be, and do not fade indistinguishably into the general population of any Pack.

From the Outside:

When dealing with a Pack, if it is positive, don't question it. Meaning, if you regularly interact with a group of women even though you do not share the same connection they do, consider yourself lucky. Sometimes, it is more beneficial to be Pack-associated than Pack-committed. If it continues to be a good thing, enjoy it. Now, if you are dealing with a group of women who are determined to give you hell, do not feel overwhelmed. Try not to absorb the weight of their attack. They are only women, not super-powerful enemies of destruction; treat them as such.

You do not have to associate with everyone in the Pack equally. If there are women whom you enjoy the company of who have relationships with other women that you don't like, maintain those connections. The key to ensuring that this friendship does not become a point of contention is to keep it pure. Keep it focused on those who are in it, not those who are not. Do not waste one another's time talking about the women you do not get along with. It puts your mutual friend in an awkward, and toxic, situation, and it cheapens the relationship you have.

I know it can be borderline impossible to pass up on a good piece of gossip about women you don't like. Especially if you are a former member of that Pack. The thirst for vindication makes knowing they may not be doing as well feel like something others need to know. It isn't. While karma may be working on them, it can just as quickly turn and humble you for your ways. Stay in your lane, stay in your friendship, and keep a healthy distance from the drama that being nosy and petty can bring.

Never follow the leader. It can be intimidating dealing with a group of women whom you are at odds with. Whether it is three or thirty, you are outnumbered, and it can be scary. It can make you question whether standing up for yourself is worth standing alone. It can make you envious of the same people whom you don't want to deal with. It can temporarily make you forget the reasons why you decided to not be a part of the Pack in the first place, and seek re-acceptance in that amnesiac state. Fight the urge to get along. Be brave against all those conflicting thoughts, and remember that who you are cannot exist with what they are.

Don't be fooled. When a Pack is toxic, everyone is miserable from top to bottom. I don't care how many group pictures they post, how many memes they share, or how loud the scream "kumbaya." They cannot exist within an unhealthy situation and be that damn happy. Not authentically. They can pretend. They can settle. They can hope, dream, and wish. You are watching the product of a lot of effort to promote the illusion that they are enjoying themselves way more than they actually are. Even if you are on a quest to be an actress, that isn't the kind of method acting you need. They will only pay you in stress and disappointment. Stand your ground. Avoid those headaches and wrinkles. Do not assimilate.

When all else fails, **break them down**. Without mercy, without hesitation, without regret, whenever you need to, break these women all the way down! What this looks like depends on the situation. If you have already distanced yourself from this group and they aren't able to reach you with their energy, just keep shining. Life can really be that easy. For most cases, just being happy in your life is all you must do to keep the Pack in their place. Once they realize the most they can do is discuss you amongst themselves, that those they tried to poison against you are uninterested, and that all they get to do is watch you be happy... Bam! You won despite their best efforts to interrupt your glow.

By investing the energy they want from you in yourself, and never giving them the response they're so desperately seeking, you take all the power from them. Toxic Packs need continuous turmoil to function. Remember, it is only having a mutual enemy that unites them. Refuse to be their enemy and watch them struggle to find themselves without you as a defining factor. This is the ideal way to deal with the Pack. It requires nothing from you other than continued greatness.

What happens if you are not in a situation that allows you to passively break them down? Fight for yourself. If someone is threatening you physically or abusing you emotionally, take the proper steps to protect yourself. That may include alerting a school counselor or your parents. That may mean documenting their threats and filing an official report. That may mean getting your black belt and posting the ceremony to your live feed.

Whenever a group of women present a tangible danger to you, you do not have to go through it alone. Seek the assistance of allies and those who are able to moderate, interfere, or reprimand those involved. Bullying is real. Being pressed by a Pack is not something you have to endure alone or for eternity. If you must address them one by one, do so. If you can engage them all at once, great. Help is out there. Use your resources to fortify yourself. Then, break them down.

Dear Packs,

Sincere connections trump dependency every time. No matter what role you play in The Pack, you still need other people to play their role in order to continue existing. There are so many conditions required to maintain your dysfunction… how do you plan on keeping it all together? If your leader leaves you, what will you do? If your followers find something shinier to admire, who will you be? At some point, the relationship needs more keeping it together than just negativity. You are already toxic on your own; do you think adding this group dynamic is in your best interest?

My only hope is that more women recognize how strong they are against you, despite you, and without you. Having friends is great. Having a group of friends is even better. But you? You are the combination of support and destruction that holds no value in the realm of womanhood. Understand that you are on borrowed time. Your strength will fade, your numbers will dwindle, your need for drama and disruption will ruin you from the inside outward, and the world will be a better place for it. No one will mourn your absence. They say any organization, team, or group is only as strong as their weakest member. You should be worried.

THE BULLY

Toxic Tip: Superman had Kryptonite, Achilles had his heel. No one is safe.

Her Toxic Range: "Spinelli 'Recess'" to "Nancy 'the Craft'"

We hate her and love her at the same time. We get a kick out of her fearless, take charge attitude, but grate our teeth at her uncouth behavior. You find yourself saying, "Yea she's bitchy, but...," as if there is any real justification after that. Sure, she is kind to you, but do you really enjoy watching her belittle others? I asked my young niece what would make her not want to be friends with someone. She responded, "If she was mean to me or other people." Isn't it great she already has the tenacity to not want to be associated with someone who has that conduct? It leaves us older girls with less of an excuse to accept or celebrate that behavior in our own lives.

Typically, the Bully is most comfortable being the Persuader of a Pack of meek women, because the weaker the woman, the less likely she will question the Bully's actions. Her existence is bolstered by those who support her behavior. We all remember the group dynamics in

Mean Girls. While it was presented in an entertaining fashion, it is a pretty unanimous belief that Regina George's bullying was unacceptable. So why are we watching our friends do the same? Why do we accept that "fetch" will never catch?

Not all Alpha Females are Bullies, but every Bully is an Alpha Female. Even if she isn't an Alpha Female amongst other Alpha Females, all she needs is one Beta to secure her Bully status. Bullies are Competitors on a power trip. Being superior isn't enough. That superiority is only purposeful if it can be used as a weapon. Bullies operate with the mindset of domination and subjugation at the same time. Unless both are present, you are not dealing with a true Bully.

Guilty by Association

Nneka's friend Chioma is the chillest person in the world when it is just the two of them. They laugh and talk about everything. Chioma is completely considerate and loving. However, the moment they are in mixed company, that awesome woman who is the first person to tell her "great job" is also the first to look for ways to demean other women.

No matter what the scenario is, Chioma will find a way to attack the other women in her presence. She makes timid women uncomfortable by talking over them or giving them no space to exist beyond her critiques. With more boisterous and energetic women, she would compete for the spotlight. If she was unable to monopolize the conversation she would nitpick their appearance, belittle their opinion, or talk badly about them to Nneka.

Nneka couldn't reconcile the two personalities that occupied the same space within Chioma. She seemed so confident and happy when they were together, but her constant confrontations reeked of desperation and insecurity. Nneka tried to laugh it off. She tried to change to subject. She tried refocusing on having a good time. But

Chioma was having a good time. She was enjoying the battle. She needed to see defeat in other women's eyes to ensure she was seen victorious on every level, all the time. Every occasion they were in public became an opportunity for confrontation, and Nneka fell less in love with the woman she considered her friend.

Spending time with her became suffocating. Nneka couldn't have any fun while Chioma spread unhappiness, so they spent more time alone. She saw the way Chioma looked at other women, always deliberately dissecting them. She also saw the way women looked at Chioma, with disgust and annoyance. She couldn't imagine being on either end of those gazes. But she already was. There was no way those women did not see her in the same negative light they saw Chioma in. Her smiles from afar, her attempts to play mediator or buffer, did not reduce her participation. She was complacent. She was an accomplice. She was responsible. She was a Bully.

Chioma wasn't a great person if she wasn't a great person. Chioma sought conflict and she prospered in an environment that Nneka didn't want to be in. It was intimidating to think about confronting Chioma. She was terrified of the backlash and knew Chioma had the potential to become extremely nasty. She was too afraid of what would happen if she ended their friendship and decided being a semi-distant acquaintance was safer than being a close foe.

One of the benefits of friendship is having a safe place to keep your innermost insecurities and secrets. The assumption is that they will not only be guarded as precious cargo but also treated with respect. Having a friend dig into her arsenal of information you shared in confidence over the span of the relationship to hurt you is one of the most vicious attacks that can occur within our friendships. She is directly using power that you have given her as a weapon against you.

Anyone who bullies you with your own feelings is one of the most toxic people that you have allowed near you. Where most people see confidential information as a privilege, she sees it as ammunition to be used at her convenience. Since you fear this loose cannon is liable to share your exploits, you remain her friend. Otherwise the code of secrecy will be discarded. You stay imprisoned in a toxic relationship because you trusted someone and now you no longer can. You know one screen shot or one status can stand between you and social humiliation. If you ask yourself what choice you have but to remain associated with the woman who has enough dirt on you to bury you more than six feet, you're being bullied.

Bully, Bullier, Bulliest

Roxanne's friend Samantha left her PE shorts at home. Since Roxanne had an extra pair, she loaned them to her so she didn't get in trouble. Samantha promised to wash the shorts and return them the next day. When Samantha finally returned the shorts to Roxanne, instead of being freshly washed, they had been written all over in permanent marker. In addition to it being disrespectful, considering Roxanne did her a favor in the first place, it was hurtful that Samantha had damaged her property for giggles. Roxanne immediately let Samantha know that not only was she pissed off, but she also fully expected to be reimbursed. Samantha brushed Roxanne off, but Roxanne persisted.

After a week of daily reminders, Samantha had her friend Rylee, a known Bully, approach Roxanne. Together they attempted to intimidate Roxanne into no longer expecting Samantha to repay her for the shorts. Roxanne was not interested in getting into a fight with Rylee, but she wasn't going to let Samantha get away with what she had done either. She had done all she could to fix the situation, but Samantha calling in her "muscle" changed the dynamic of the exchange, and Roxanne had to find alternative ways to defend herself and get compensation for her damaged goods.

Roxanne's older sister Jolene attended the same school. She informed her sister of the situation and Rylee's implied threat. Jolene did not take too fondly to hearing how her little sister was being treated. The next day Roxanne, Jolene, and Jolene's friend all confronted Samantha and Rylee together. Without fighting our arguing, their unified presence was enough of a reminder that every Bully has her limit. In this case, the limit was Jolene and her friend. Roxanne's shorts were quickly replaced, with both Samantha and Rylee being nothing but cordial afterward.

What kind of power does a Bully have if it is conditional? None. They weren't ordained from birth to be in charge. They weren't elected to be the ruler of anything. They don't possess some unobtainable skill that cannot be matched. These are regular girls and women who have lost their way and think they will find it by walking over others. We allow them to believe that their toxicity is a superpower instead of a super flaw. We allow them to believe their toxicity is a strength instead of a weakness. We allow them to believe that they can control us instead of requiring them to control themselves. Bullies are made by the actions, or inactions, of all those around them. They do not exist without our confirmation. We are the real bullies because we allow it. We are assigning another woman the privilege of hurting us, when that is not a right she needs or deserves.

How to Deal with a Bully

Dealing with Bullies can be difficult for so many reasons. Not only are they dedicated to the thought of bringing us down, they rarely volunteer to be brought down to size. When your method of madness is crushing those below you, you rarely show your vulnerabilities enough for them to figure out a methodology to defeat you.

Just like how you deal with the Pack, you must face a Bully head on. This can feel worse than the mistreatment, for those who avoid confrontation as much as possible. You can ignore a Bully and hope your lack of involvement encourages her to find a more susceptible target, but you're not doing they next person a favor by passing on that toxicity. Bullies may never change their mentality, but they do need to be reminded that their actions can be acknowledged, addressed, and admonished.

You cannot give Bullies free reign to ruin your life or the lives of others. Their energy is dangerous, even to those who are not directly being bullied. Stand firm against them. If you find it impossible to do so alone, do not hesitate to recruit like-minded women to stand against them. A unified front is much harder to intimidate or manipulate. Protecting yourself and protecting others means not standing silent if you see someone else being hurt. That is what the Bully wants: your silence. Don't give them the freedom of your fear.

Dear Bullies,

Let's talk about the secret we both know. You're not that bad. You know it and I know it. That is why you spend so much time trying to convince the world you are. You have the potential to be a leader, but you would rather be a boss. You could move women upward, but you would rather push them down so you can feel higher.

Despite knowing this, for some reason, I want to gently reassure you that you don't need to be so hard to be valued. You would be just as important if you didn't force everyone to tell you that you are. But I know that I cannot be gentle with you. My words would fall on deaf ears. You are unable to absorb the possibility of power without preeminence because you do not see the separation between the two. You do not respect softness; you take advantage of it. You want to manipulate it and use it to further your ascension.

You need to know that you can still be in control and be kind. But you already know that. You are aware of the opportunity to be liked and have decided that the benefits of being feared outweigh the risks of losing your likability. That is why I cannot handle you delicately. I can't try to rationalize that you are anything but the Bully you are. You do not deserve the niceties that you refuse to give others. You do not deserve the courtesy of tenderness. You attack with delight. You wound with pleasure. You harm intentionally and recklessly for no other reason other than it makes you feel good. You should be fully recognized for those malicious efforts.

Eventually one of two things will happen. Either those you hurt will realize their strength and defeat you, or you will meet a stronger and harder woman who will Bully you back. You deserve both of those fates. I hope you rethink whether inflicting pain, feeding off the pain of others, and requiring their pain to appease your own toxic need is the best way to live. Sis, it isn't.

THE DRAMA QUEEN

Toxic Tip: Are you comfortable with an audience of one?

Range: "I have a paper cut. Do you have a Band-Aid?" to "No one liked my Facebook status yet. Just kill me now."

Her life is like a poorly written made for TV movie. As her friend we get the joy (*cough* sarcasm), of watching every act whenever we are around her. Instead of getting the hijinks and hilarity of a comedy, we get the monologues and redundant story lines of a soap opera. Everything occurs at a heightened sense of excitement or despair.

So that B-plus on the Econ test will now be the source of her woe for the next two days. As if you didn't get a B-minus. Every nail break, break up, and day at work is a production. While she enjoys the attention and the drama, we are wishing for the closing call, and silently hoping that the main character gets knocked off in the next installation so we don't have to watch the sequel.

If being a Drama Queen is her occupation, then drama-starting is her hobby. They go hand and hand. Exactly how did we end up getting into a club brawl? Oh yes! She needed to argue with the girl in the bathroom over who was next in line. We weren't, by the way. Those bad vibes followed us to the dance floor, and it didn't take long before her eye rolls and flinging elbows started an all-out fight. Typical. We love our girl, but Geesh! How much hoopla can one person take? She takes things so far that it is hard to have a normal relationship, where you both get your fair share of the limelight.

Keep the Drama for Ya Mama

Shana's friend Brittani loves to talk about how she is too busy living life and growing her empire, whatever that means, to be involved in the banality of conflict. Yet every single one of her posts is a meme or story about interactions with the same theme: drama. If she is not calling out another woman for subbing her, while hypocritically returning the sub, she is talking to the masses, reminding them of a litany of flaws. Shana was duped into believing Brittani was a cool person because their interactions only happened in person when they occasionally met up.

After friending her on Facebook and getting constantly bombarded with the exact drama Brittani claimed to be avoiding, Shana tried to understand her differing points of view. The more time she spent with her, the more she realized that her representation online is the real her. Between Brittani's obvious boredom and loneliness, she regularly used the likes and comments on social media to provide not just her entertainment for the day, but also much of her everyday interaction.

When Shana and Brittani were together, their conversation was more spent going over the drama created from Brittani's posts and less actually enjoying one another's time. Should Shana not respond immediately to Brittani's text or call, she too would be the subject of an indirect status. Their relationship became more consuming than Shana ever thought possible. Shana believed the catalyst for her issues with Brittani centered on her social media use. So, when she unfollowed, much of her annoyance with Brittani also disappeared.

When Brittani needed to spend an extended amount of time staying with Shana, their friendship reached a critical tipping point. With Brittani occupying her space, and interacting with her on a constant basis, Shana saw all the extended scenes of her constant battle with life. Nothing ever just happened with Brittani.

Every situation was met with an eager response to extend the friction or frustration. There was constant yelling at anyone and everyone whom she could get to listen. The same post Shana tried to avoid reading was living and breathing toxicity in her living room. Shana couldn't pinpoint exactly how Brittani managed to seem so normal before, because she was showing out now and Shana just wanted to return to a less exhausting existence.

Drama Queens can be sneaky. They know from experience that most people tire of their shenanigans quickly, so they often portray themselves as the exact opposite. They sport titles like drama-free in their Instagram bios and profess over and over how little time they have to take in the negativity of others. We are drawn to them because that is exactly what we are looking for: a Mary J. Blige circa 2001 type of life. We have grown into the people we are comfortable being, and we look to exist with other women who enjoy life more than strife.

As The Drama Queens become more comfortable with us, they start cracking. They can't help themselves. They can only pretend so long, after all. They start smiling less and griping more. Not because they feel so close to us that they are now unafraid to show us their vulnerabilities, but because they know we have a connection with them and they are ready to start the show.

We all have moments with irrational responses and unwarranted, heightened reactions. She is not this person. She legit has only one mode of operation: too much. If we had known beforehand this is what we were signing up for, we would have declined, but she hid all the "extraness" in the fine print of the terms and conditions, and we are now stuck in an undesirable friendship contract.

Wait, What Happened?

Nicole and Leila's relationship can teeter on toxic at times, but overall, Nicole considered Leila good people. Eventually their friendship started to hit more snags than ever. They bumped heads in competition or contradiction of everything. They got to the point that they no longer spoke to each other outside of pleasant greetings.

It was hurtful for Nicole, but she resigned herself to the fact that it was probably for the best. Soon after their relationship dissolved, Nicole noticed mutual acquaintances they once shared now treating her differently. They were more distant or sometimes whispered when she came around. She couldn't figure out the reason for the sudden change in climate for multiple friendships.

Since nothing ever stays a secret long, many of these shared friends started to let tidbits of information slip. Sometime shortly after she and Leila stopped being friends, Leila went on a smear campaign to establish herself as the person wronged in the friendship. Nicole couldn't imagine how their mutual decision to stop their corroding relationship turned into a storyline. She and Leila both seemed content with just being amiable. Nicole had no bad blood towards Leila. They just grew apart.

It made no sense to Nicole that she was finding out through second and third parties about Leila's exaggerated or completely fabricated story. Just because they weren't besties anymore didn't mean they had to be enemies. They most certainly didn't need to be fighting for the loyalty of their remaining friends or creating drama where it didn't previously exist. Nicole did her best to deflect or defend herself against some of the rumors that were now circulating. Ultimately she ended up losing additional friends because Leila made it her duty to strike first and strike hard.

Nicole never had any intention of discussing their friendship, or its ending, with other people. Their friends saw the issues as clearly as they did, without having to highlight them in yellow. But Leila, missing the excitement that their contention brought to her life, needed to continue it even after the friendship was over... whether Nicole liked it or not.

Sometimes the Drama Queen doesn't have the personality to carry on a production all by herself, so she does the next best thing. She directs the show. She's a Gossip. This isn't your everyday gossip, either. I am a fan of a little juicy every now and then. But if every drop of information she gets ends up reaching the far edges of civilization, chances are she's not the one you want to confide in.

But why would a close friend abandon the laws of friendship so quickly, just to tell the world something you clearly shared with her in confidence? Easy, it's the excitement of the reaction. We need air to breath and a gossip needs drama to survive. She revels in her role as the go-to person for dirt. And she will deliver everything she knows, loyalties be damned. Attention becomes more important than your relationship, and what is shared between you becomes fuel for her toxicity.

This fuel includes when she gets into an argument or issue with you. Many of us discuss our relationship issues with other friends. That, in itself, isn't unhealthy. Going to a buffer to discuss your ideas and feelings is a helpful way to not only vent but also work through emotions, so that when you talk to the friend you are upset with, you have an idea as to how you want to approach the situation. You have a moment to calm down. You have a moment to analyze yourself and your own fault in the issue.

A gossiping Drama Queen is talking to someone else to have something to talk about. She has no interest in actually giving advice or assistance to work through these issues with you. Should someone make the mistake of coming to her in hopes of falling on a free shoulder or receiving open ears, they'll find someone less interested in being the voice of reason, and more interested in giving them a reason to keep the animosity going. The Drama Queen doesn't always center the drama around herself. If ever she cannot get that close to the action, she will happily settle for watching it all unfold from the audience.

How to Deal with a Drama Queen

There are Organic Drama Queens and GMO Drama Queens. With an Organic Drama Queen, even though it seems implausible, her dramatics are an accurate representation of her emotions. She is not intentionally seeking direct responses; she just cannot control the extravagance of her actions. The reaction she gets to her extreme displays is not always what she wants. If someone gets hurt or angry because of what she has done or said, she isn't happy about it. It just won't stop her from repeating it. Her toxicity is compulsive. It is more difficult to deal with this type of Drama Queen because she's not vindictive, but she is often more than you can handle.

When dealing with an Organic Drama Queen, whom you can clearly see has great intentions wrapped in an overzealous personality, take a break from her, whether physical or mental. Every action of hers does not warrant a reaction from you. There is little you can do to restrict who she is; however, you can alter your investment and your perception of her. Depriving her of your response will also give her the opportunity to focus on her responses, and she will learn how to navigate her feelings. Let your inaction and silence give her the space to see the results of her expression first hand.

Now with the GMO Drama Queen, the woman who formulates, creates, organizes, and distributes unnecessary drama to the world, call cut on her. The ones that are less toxic and more bored may realize that they are not going to be tolerated or included because of their actions. That could be just enough of a deterrent for them to find healthier ways to use their energy.

For the wonderful UPS (Universal Petty Services) ladies, who have a history, an addiction, and a need to keep the drama brewing and reproducing, stop giving them content. You must also stop receiving their information. It will let you know whether you enjoy their drama and if that is the real reason you are associated with them, or if you still have something more significant unifying you. Determining the Drama Queen's purpose in your life is the first step to knowing if you're merely a consumer or a contributor to her toxic behavior.

Dear Drama Queens,

It can be hard to close the curtains on yourself; trust me I know, but sometimes the run is just over. Other people need a moment to feel significant. Not everyone wants to be constantly outdone. You may be thinking you never go out of your way to do this, and you could be right. But you also never go out of your way to make sure you do not overshadow everyone. If it is their birthday, and for all of the evening you have usurped the talking time, intentional or not, you just made your best friend the understudy at her own celebration. Now you know that ain't right. If you were really as dynamic as you think you are, you would know when the right time is to turn it up and when the situation dictates you to dial it down. You become toxic when you forget to remember that your friendship is about two people, not just you and your emotions.

That advice does not extend to you conniving and shameful Drama Queens that are wreaking havoc and leaving a trail of disaster wherever you go. When you start shit for the sake of starting it, when you set people up to get their feelings hurt because you need something to do, when you break the trust of a friend because you don't have anything else better to talk about, you don't deserve to be called friend.

You need to really assess what qualities you have outside of your open mouth always vomiting someone else's business. Who you are outside of what information you have gets lost in the transmission. You're in a world where women are seeking other women to live life with, not seeking journalists to give the inside scoop. Decide who you really you want to be. Are you the homie or are you *TMZ*? Are you interesting, or do you just have something interesting to reveal? Are you a friend or a microphone? Are you healthy or are you toxic?

THE LOVE ENTHUSIAST

Toxic Tip: All things are *not* fair in love and war.

Range: "I think I like him," to "I love him so much, I can't think without him."

Could we be any more obsessed with love? We are so preoccupied with the need to fill a hole that doesn't exist that we create a hole that doesn't exist. If harnessed, the amount of energy that is given to romance could provide electricity for the world. To exclude this from our conversation about our own relationships would be neglecting a large part of our natural dynamic. It is not our only, or the most important, problem, but it is often a problem.

I had a hard time deciding how to attack this subject without overstaying my welcome. There are just so many different types of Love Enthusiasts out here.

I am going to place the most prevalent personalities into their own toxic subgroups:

- Forever

- Equal Opportunity
- Questionable

There are many other types, but to discuss them all would be a book in itself. Let's get to work understanding how our quest for love can hinder and harm love that we have already found with one another.

The Forever Enthusiast

This is the woman who is always Noah's Ark-ing. She infrequently finds herself outside of a relationship. During the rare occasions she is unattached, she shows all the attributes of friendship that remind you why she became your bestie in the first place… only to revert to ghosting you the moment she resettles back into her coupled-up community. It's disrespectful and it is hurtful. The Forever Enthusiast's focus never strays long from her goal of being somebody's somebody. But you don't have to be second fiddle. She should treat you as an important person in her life regardless of whoever else is there. That is the optimal situation, but frankly, it does not always play out so well.

Un-pause Us

There is nothing more unfortunate than losing a relationship in order to gain another. Especially because it can be prevented. However, that is exactly what happens when Sasha forgets to be proactive in maintaining friendship ties with Kelly. Regularly, Sasha finds love and becomes so engrossed in her relationship that she neglects all the wonderful women who loved her beforehand, including Kelly. Sasha must know she is wrong, right? Kelly wonders how she can be so blinded.

Sasha doesn't just exchange their Tuesday dance classes for Netflix & Chill with him. She also manages to forget to text, call, email, or smoke signal. She doesn't seem to remember Kelly still exists. To add insult to injury, in the rare times Kelly does get to see or talk to her, the conversation always manages to find its way back to her current relationship. And as if it could not get any more offensive, while Kelly talks about her latest milestone, Sasha isn't paying attention. She's too busy messaging her boyfriend. Funny how her multitasking skills are so sharp now.

Kelly is genuinely happy for her to be in the relationship she desires. Now that she has what she wants, Sasha doesn't want to rain on her love parade. But she feels abandoned. And rightfully so. She just doesn't know how to approach the subject without losing the little piece of friendship she has left. Kelly is pretty sure that when she referenced Sasha as her Best Friend Forever, there wasn't an "or until I find a man" clause mentioned. Yet here they are on this toxic teeter-totter of who is wrong and right when all she really wants is her friend back.

How to Deal with a Forever Enthusiast

Do not make allowances for a friend who decides that her love bubble is a valid reason to go ghost. We all need to stop giving these universal passes for this unacceptable behavior because we secretly hope to be given the same pass in the future. We need to hold each other accountable for the promises that we share. Then maybe, just maybe, we can stop pretending that our partnerships are the problem. The Forever Enthusiast needs to understand she can't be flighty with her words and actions and then turnaround and expect your undying love and affection. When you have friends, that is how you treat them. As friends.

Call a spade a spade. If she finds herself unable to uphold her end of the friendship once she is committed, then she is choosing to abandon it. Sometimes we avoid declaring that fact because it will hurt too much. It does not feel good to be tossed aside, regardless of the reason.

But how she treats you before, during, and after her relationships is her choice. Now you must make a choice regarding how you choose to proceed from that point.

Dear Forever Enthusiasts,

It can be difficult to remember who needs more time and attention and whom you've already checked off your "to friend" list. But it is completely possible. Stop pretending you can't make it to movie night, or you're too busy to check-in. Your selfie you just posted on Snapchat says otherwise. It takes literally ten seconds to let a friend know you're thinking about them. Do that during the time you convince yourself that you don't have enough of it to care.

What happens if that precious little bubble you've decided to stay in bursts? I should hope you don't expect the friends you've starved of your friendship to run to your bedside and nurse you back to health. Even in the best-case scenario, that love grows into marriage and even family. Who are you sharing your life with? Who is throwing your bridal shower or babysitting for you on a much-needed date night? Not your support system. You no longer have one. You traded and upgraded, remember? The model of life you're choosing doesn't come standard with those additions. Instead of seamlessly intertwining your boo into the fabric of your life, you discarded the close-knit ties to build a brand-new blanket. You have made that bed, you deserve to lie in it, freeze in it, or toss and turn in the loneliness you created for yourself.

Equal Opportunity Enthusiast

There is a certain freedom that you have when you're in the dating world. Some of the best times I had were when me and my girls were out on the prowl, looking for love or just a good time, sometimes, in all the wrong places. While the "right one" eludes us, we can make toxic love decisions that throw our hearts and existing relationships into turmoil.

The issue with having a friend who is an Equal Opportunity Enthusiast is you never know what their limits are, or if they have any. Every moment is the perfect moment to risk it all for Love. These are the women who have deemed themselves the Robin Hood of Love and throw themselves at everything that moves… and the ones who pretend they do not notice the bling on their ring finger.

You shouldn't have to worry that you are going to be left ride-less over the possibility that she gets to hook up with Guy A.

You shouldn't have to cover for her hooking up with someone else while she is dating Guy B.

You shouldn't have to worry about leaving her in a room alone with Guy C, after you've already established that he's your guy.

When a friend tends to put lust potential before everything else on a consistent basis, it makes us question whether anything, their careers, their passions, their family, or their friends, can ever compete. Wanting love is great. Working to keep it is essential. However, sacrificing all else for a glimpse, that may not actually be a glimpse, every single time… toxic.

That's Not Your Toy

Toya's friend Candice is like much like herself, single and ready to do more than just mingle. They are both hoping to be in serious relationships and understand that navigating the dating world means finding their prince among the frogs. Toya soon realizes there is a definite difference between hers and Candice's approach to the end goal. She's not immune to a drunken hookup. In her lonelier moments, she has entertained the possibility of a relationship with someone she knows she's not compatible with. It is not her usual way of handling her love life, but things happen. With every bump in the road, she reevaluates and redirects herself to healthier and more productive efforts.

Candice, on the other hand, continuously gets herself into messy situations. She knows what she is initiating will be a hindrance to her happiness and still proceeds to participate even though it will blow up in her face. Any warm body in her bed, her old flame or someone's new heat, satisfies her need to feel she is not alone. Part of Toya understands. It is hard to be a single in a world that tells you you need to be a double to achieve ultimate happiness. But Candice's lack of concern for anyone but herself every time she makes these harmful decisions can't be justified as just "scratching an itch."

Toya wants to not judge Candice harshly, but she finds herself criticizing her actions regularly. She starts to lack sympathy when the inevitable heartbreak occurs. She finds her impulsive actions reckless and disrespectful. Toya tries to maintain her friendship by focusing on all things not male related. But after a few drinks, the subject always leads to another story about conquest that should have been avoided. Toya begins to wonder, "If Candice is willing to disrespect herself and other people by engaging in relationships with involved men, will she do the same to me? Can I trust her around my future beau? Are these questions I should have to ask about my friend?"

How to Deal with an Equal Opportunity Enthusiast

If you are in a serious relationship, how do you deal with a friend who is dating a person already in a committed relationship? While you may not have directly dealt with this type of situation, you probably know someone who is the other woman. You'll have a friend or coworker explain to you the sordid details of their exploits with men who belonged to other women. So, if you are in the process of planning your dream wedding while listening half-heartedly to your friend gripe about a man she should not be involved with anyway, what can you do? The parallel is too close to not be affected. Now you have found yourself in a situation where your morals or feelings are at odds with your friend's decisions.

Stand by your values. That does not mean you must berate your friend and go out of your way to make her feel as bad as you see her. It can mean avoiding conversations about her love life altogether. Once you have stated your opinion just once, you are not obligated to assuage her guilt by pretending to give her support in her actions. You've already addressed it. After that, if you can, you avoid it. If it is thrown in your face, when she feels the need to share despite your best efforts, you ignore it. Maybe this is just a phase, and you want to love her through it. That is commendable and very friendly of you. But you don't have to do so at the cost of yourself. Friends do not ask you to sacrifice your morals for their destruction.

You may decide that you are so against what she is going that you cannot interact with her if she continues the relationship. That is okay too. We are only responsible for ourselves. When the path she is on includes some of your deal breakers along the way, you have every right to walk away. You don't have to be toxified by her actions.

Dear Equal Opportunity Enthusiasts,

If you're stepping out on your man, pick a side. You're either in or out. Let us know when you decide whether you want to be faithful or not. Until then leave us out of your drama. For those throwing their love around all willy-nilly at any Tom, Dick, or Harry regardless of their relationship status, knock it off. If you're the other woman, throw the whole side chick mentality away. I initially stayed away from using that phrase because it is used and glorified so often that it doesn't feel like the slur it should be.

Just so there is no confusion, I am not using that word kindly, or mildly. When you assume you're the only person affected by what you do, you flippantly dismiss the life of the other woman involved and absolve the guilt of the pain you're inflicting. You are ruining lives and relationships. Knock it off.

Your friends who say they are not judging you are lying. We are all judging you, harshly. You're making your friends question not just your character but also theirs for associating with you. You make us question your respect for us, your ability to make sound decisions, and your love for yourself. I know women like you. Not one of them can be in a room with my husband alone. Ever. I won't apologize for it either. When it comes to men, you make bad decisions. Be a better woman to all women and DO BETTER!

The Questionable Enthusiast

They're not the right person for her, and you know it. What can you do? I would be setting you up for failure if I led you to believe that sensibility will override any hurt feelings from your disapproval. Probability is fifty-fifty at best that if you have a major gripe about your friend's boo, you will walk away victorious hand in hand with your friend. We lose our friends too quickly to love. Not always by the act of falling; sometimes by the act of staying. Their decision to stay with their love interest over understanding your concern can be like a stab in the heart. All we wanted was the best for them, and somehow, we lost them.

It can be impossible to understand why our friends turn against or dismiss us when we are trying to help. We sit there with egg on our face for extending our arm in assistance. Try to remember that being mistreated is bad enough. But being mistreated publicly is just downright embarrassing. Not everyone can handle the shame of being wronged. Therefore, they get defensive, refute, ignore, and do everything but admit they aren't with the right person. Anything, including losing you, to keep their relationship contained. And it will suck every single time.

There will be times you have to handle your friend's relationships with the delicacy of a bomb squad. Love is a sensitive emotion that likes to be coddled and caressed. We run a very real risk of damaging our friendships with our perception of their romantic relationships. If you thought she was only marginally interested when she was actually falling head over heels, you can be too vocal too soon with your disdain for her new Sig O and find yourself at opposite ends of their relationship, and your friendship.

Keep This Between Us

Gabby knows some salacious dirt about Araceli's boyfriend. She knows from a very reliable source that he has cheated on her. She feels it is her responsibility to tell her, but the person who gave her the information did so with the specific instructions she not share it with Araceli. She can't see how she can keep the information from Araceli, and she can't see how she can share it without jeopardizing her other friendship. All she wants at this point is to not know what she knows.

Gabby asks a mutual friend for advice, and she confirms what Gabby already accepted. She cannot withhold this precious intelligence. If Araceli finds out later that she knew a crucial piece of information and didn't disclose it, Gabby runs the risk of losing their friendship. This is a lose-lose situation for Gabby, with the only benefit that if she tells Araceli, she can retain her title as a good friend. Considering her options, she decides that she'll have to accept the possibility it that will all blow up in her face, but she will tell Araceli.

As soon as Gabby tells Araceli what she has heard, instead of thanking her for the information, Araceli begins to question and vilify the person Gabby found out from. Gabby considers the source as much of a friend as Araceli and defends both the person and the information they provided. Araceli remains adamant that this is all a coordinated effort to destroy her relationship out of jealousy. Gabby tries to reason with Araceli and convince her that it is love and concern motivating her to share the information. However, it falls on deaf ears. Araceli chooses to believe her man and admonishes Gabby for interfering. Gabby has known Araceli for years. She has been there for the beginnings and endings of her other relationships without ever causing any issues. Why would Araceli think she was trying to hurt her?

Soon after, Araceli tells her boyfriend of the accusations. The information comes full circle, through the person who told Gabby back to Gabby … just as she feared, but expected, it would. Everyone is upset with Gabby, and all she has to fall back on is that she was being a good friend. Great. She's a good friend. With no friends to show for it.

How to Deal with a Questionable Enthusiast

There are women who have walked their "Miss" friends down the aisle, and then are no longer friends with the "Mrs." It was not the wedding that made their friendship falter. It was the bride not wanting to be subjected to her friend's dissatisfaction with her choice of groom. Whether or not the Mrs. eventually agrees with the bleak opinion of him will matter less the more she believes that she cannot change it. She may look back four years from now and realize that her friend clairvoyantly predicted her relationship's dismal outcome, or she can look back after those same four years and be completely content with her happily ever after.

Since you cannot look predict the future to know how things will pan out, the best tactic is to be mindful of the what, how, and when of your words. It may be the only way you can keep her as a friend

If your friend asks you what you think about her new guy, play it neutral until you have a good idea about her feelings toward him. This will allow time to put her current attachment and future relationship goals into perspective. There is no reason to stage an intervention if she only plans on hooking up with him. Reserve that effort for when there is a real threat. Unless you know him personally, and more so then she does, your opinion is just that: an opinion. If you don't have facts backing up that gut feeling that he will mess up her credit as bad as her heart, don't divulge that information, yet.

We are so concerned for our friends that we don't just assume we know what is best for them; we feel it is our duty to protect them. However, your responsibility is to support her, not necessarily her relationship. You cannot choose her match for her, so do not try. If he is a bad guy, he will eventually reveal himself for what he is, and she will be able to see it first-hand. There is no need to set yourself up early for an "I told you so" moment. It won't be as gratifying as you think.

If you must share pertinent information, do so delicately. The trick to informing your friend, while leaving no question of your intention, is to deliver the information without emotion or attachment. You don't say, "He is a dog because he cheated on his last girlfriend." Instead you say, "He did cheat on his last girlfriend. I don't know if he's still that guy, but he used to be." Then give her the opportunity to absorb and respond before bombarding her with more information. Let her make the choice to ask for additional details. It will be difficult to hold your tongue, but value your relationship with her more than stopping her relationship with him.

Lastly, if, despite holding in your gut feeling and giving her substantial warnings, she is still dedicated to this poor excuse for a boyfriend, you cannot use every time he messes up as a door to walk through and deliver your thoughts about him. *When* is still key. If you want honor that heavy badge of friendship, even during these times, you will have to censor yourself. You must continue to remember that this isn't about you. Even if your front row seats have you as invested as you would be if you were in her shoes, if she does not ask your opinion, do not give it.

This includes when she is openly venting. Discussing how you feel with your friend does not always mean you are looking to hear what they have to say. Often it will feel that her venting is, in fact, the very invitation you have been waiting for. But sadly, it isn't. Your invitation is her asking your opinion.

Until that formal declaration of assistance leaves her lips, stick with safe mm-hmms, I sees, and I understands. If you feel you will absolutely explode playing a mime, a beneficial way to not directly give your opinion is to ask her questions.

I do not mean questions like, "Why don't you just leave him already?"

I mean questions like, "If he says he can't stay faithful, how do you see it working beyond his infidelities?" Always lead with fact and follow up with the focus on her. This shows her you are interested in her feelings.

Now, before you once again want to throw something, when she does ask your opinion, tell her the truth. There are many ways to be truthful, so try not to go from zero to sixty the first moment you get the chance. The only thing that will accomplish is fewer requests for your input. Stay with facts before dwelling on your feeling. She should remain, even now, the focus of your conversation. This is not about how you think he is so terrible because he doesn't answer any of her calls and can never make time for her. Even if it 100 percent true. It should be that you know how much communication is important to her and that she deserves to be in a relationship with someone who prioritizes her. If he can be that person and they can work on it, awesome, as long as she is truly happy. Some days it will feel like you need the strength of an army of women to hold yourself back. But it will be worth it.

The Exceptions to the Rules

The Superwoman Exception: If your friend is in danger. The relationship is *abusive* emotionally, mentally, financially, or physically. Do not pass go. Do not collect $200. You need to immediately try to intervene. She may not be responsive. She may not listen. Whether you are appreciated in that moment isn't important. You have set yourself up as her ally and a friend she can go to if she decides she needs help. And if her relationship is legitimately dangerous, she will need your help. You may not be able to save her from her next heartbreak, but if you can try to save her from herself in the direst of situations, do so. Her safety is worth any risk.

The Broken Record: If you have stayed silent when you should, and spoken up when requested, and she is in the same situation. You do not have to continue to repeat the cycle. If she is adamant that even though her relationship could be a storyline on *Jerry Springer* she is stuck like glue, let girlfriend do her. You can only allow yourself to become involved and overworked over someone else's relationship. Your "we" does not have to include "she and he." She needs to review her priorities and dedication to your friendship, not you. I can't guarantee that you will stay her confidant in all things love-related going forward, or that you will be involved in her next journey of amour, but that may be the best thing for your friendship.

Dear All My Questionable Enthusiasts,

We are trying to love you. That's it. Why you take any criticism of your relationship as a personal attack is beyond me. You know it isn't perfect, and we aren't the bad guy for pointing that out. Handling you and your situationship like a fragile package requires too much from your friends, and we weren't trained by FedEx. Allow us to have a friendship with you that does not include your relationship with them, so we can all be happy.

If you are only committed to your person, and everyone else in your life is optional, just come right out and say it. If that is the decision you have made, and you are content with it, then you should just lead with that information. Don't make us jump through hoops and walk tightropes like circus performers, when we don't matter that much by comparison. Save us the effort and the act. Keeping us around when we are disposable is selfish and unfair.

How to Deal with All Love Enthusiasts

Beyond watching what you do, there is nothing you can do. I know that sounds anti-climactic. The truth is, if you do everything "right," things can still go wrong. Sometimes our friends just decide to move on to other phases of their lives without us. Whether we were replaced by her relationship or a combination of her boo and their circle of friends doesn't matter. We lost. I can't say it enough; yes it sucks, but move on.

It isn't healthy to hold onto something that is no longer there. It isn't healthy to hold onto the anger or the sadness that replaces it. Often the most toxic thing that comes from a relationship with a Love Enthusiast isn't what happens along the way, but the garbage of emotions and hostility that we are left to sort through after. When necessary, when nothing can be done to either come to terms with her new life or the way she operates in her current one, move on. She has made her decision. Accept it.

Dear All Love Enthusiasts,

The urban myth is that being in a relationship makes our friends sad or bitter. That their jealousy, selfishness, and inability to share our joy prevents them from seeing how important our Sweetheart really is to our happiness.

It isn't true. It is your abandonment.

It's the fact that you gave your friend a niche in your life, reinforced how significant her role is, only to negate what she contributes the moment the toy you really wanted is up for grabs. Regardless of whether it was because of he, she, or them, *no judgement*, you left your Best Friend Forever behind for the chance to have a better forever with someone else.

Chances are, your significant other has a different relationship with you than your friends do. You did not just replace her with another her. You replaced her with someone who can give you more than she can: a last name, a family, health benefits, a legal claim to your life. All things not typically covered in the friend zone. Exactly how is she supposed to feel about it? It's unfortunate we abandon our friends with much more fervor and less guilt when we categorize it as a necessity of love. But when finding the ones who will love us, we should always be adding to the equation, not subtracting.

THE VICTIM

Toxic Tip: Life is not happening to you; it is happening because of you.

Her Toxic Scale: "Got a speeding ticket for going 37 in the 35 zone; life isn't fair," to "I got probation for my role in a multi-million dollar Ponzi Scheme; life isn't fair."

The Victim is a vampire blend of toxic traits. Hollywood has invested a lot of time and dollars in selling us the idea that vampires are sexy and thrilling, but if you ask me, there is absolutely nothing sensual about having your life sucked out of you. Imagine a Drama Queen and a Pessimist had a child; their dysfunctional spawn would be the Victim. A hybrid child harnessing all the worst traits of her origin personalities in a cocktail of toxicity.

This lady is all woe-is-she! She's incapable of ever finding fault within herself. Somehow that D she got on her child development final was the fault of the professor and not her choosing to party instead of studying the night before. How could she know that it would cover the chapters that were listed in the syllabus? There are a thousand things that she could be doing to make her life better, but the responsibility of her happiness always falls squarely on someone else's shoulders.

We all have times when we are done wrong or unnecessarily dragged through the mud, but if she stays with the man who has cheated on her nine times, how could she know he would do it a tenth? This is the Victim's mentality. Her lackluster approach to responsibility and serious case of denial can quickly become an issue for any friendship. If she is hell-bent on convincing herself she has no obligation to own her actions and the consequences that come from them, how can she be a positive influence in our life? As friends, we have a duty to challenge our friends and encourage them to grow. How can she do this if she is too busy avoiding her role in her own reality? Imagine how taxing it would be to help a friend work through a problem that she cannot recognize her involvement in.

Whose Fault Is It, Anyway?

Cassie is crying to Jessica about how her fiancé left her and she doesn't know why. She tells her that he packed when she was at work and disappeared without thinking about her feelings or about the rent that would soon be due. She complains about their ruined vacation plans. It will be a hassle to get a refund for the hotel, and she doesn't know what he's going to do with their two non-refundable plane tickets. The pain, confusion, and shock of how abruptly he left is too much to bear. He could have stayed to talk things out or work on their problems.

She has Jessica deeply embedded in a web of concern and anger towards her ex-boo. How *could* he leave?! With the wedding plans in full swing?! With all the years they have invested, and all the promises made, he just leaves?! The audacity!

Oh yeah, she was also cheating on him, she finally manages to mention.

It has been going on for about six months now, with a mutual associate, and they may have been outed by another acquaintance. But he left her!

To a rational person it's glaringly obvious, that's probably the root of the breakup. However, to a Cassie, her indiscretion only occurred because he was being neglectful while working so many hours. Yes, it was to pay for her dream wedding, but she told him she hated him always being gone. Therefore, he should take that into consideration before punishing her for her moments of weakness. Jessica had to rewind and replay the information in her mind. Cassie is actively participating in a relationship outside of the relationship she is losing, but her ex-fiancé needs to be the considerate one?

Now Jessica is sitting there trying to perform mental gymnastics to figure out exactly what Cassie is confessing to and what she is actually upset about. How she could possibly justify her infidelity? How did she expect any other ending to the tragedy she orchestrated? Cassie was sitting there blubbering like she'd done nothing to deserve this moment, when she totally deserved much more than a silent departure.

But Jessica is her friend. So instead of telling her how wrong she is, she tells her it is going to be okay. That everyone could have handled things differently and how maybe they will be able to reconcile. Jessica believes none of this, but she is at a loss for words that fit without sounding cruel. She convinces herself that after some time has passed, she will really break it down to Cassie how she was the catalyst in this catastrophe. This just isn't the time.

Jessica never got around to breaking the news to Cassie. By the time the dust from that situation cleared, there was another one already on the horizon. There never seemed to be a good time to tell Cassie that she was wrong without feeling wrong about saying it, and that is what was wrong with their friendship.

How to Deal with Victims

The victim draws on your sympathy to keep you in the friendship. You're a hostage to toxic with nothing but guilt waiting for you, should you choose to walk out the door. You become a friend by force of compassion.

Let me set you free: You. Cannot. Save. Them. Stop. Trying. You cannot make anyone take responsibility for their actions or lives. Stop Trying. What the Victim wants most is for someone to keep trying to save them. Don't be that person. Stop Trying.

It is hard to distance from a Victim for many reasons. Some Victims have origin stories that pull at our heartstrings. Some have situations they are currently in that legitimately deserve the sincerest considerations. However, even tragedy has a threshold. That limit has been surpassed so many times by now that you need to learn some boundaries before you also lose your connection to logic.

That does not mean you should ignore their legitimate gripes. It means do not react when you know that what they want more than support is a way out of owning their mistakes. Make sure they know that you believe they are not just capable, but accountable, for their own decisions. If they are being worn too thin, feeling unappreciated, or unhappy with the conditions they have created for themselves, then they need to change it. Don't be the victim to the Victim. One is enough. No, one is too much. The less you play into the fantasy, the more she will have to operate like the world she occupies is one of her own creation.

Dear Victims,

I will not remain in this suspended state with you. It is too harmful to support your irresponsibility. You want to go through life without being liable for anything. I cannot understand how you think acting helpless is your most powerful position. You have to want to be the protagonist in your story and stop playing a supporting character in your life. I will not be your hero, your therapist, or your sanitation lady. You want other people to save you, fix you, and clean up after your life, but these are your jobs. It's a lot of work. I know because I already occupy those roles for myself. I don't have time to pick up extra shifts on your behalf.

Friends are there to hold your hand, lift you up, and guide you on occasion. Not to lie to you, as you lie to yourself. Not to pretend you are a better person than you are. We are not here to keep pretending there are villains that don't exist so that you can keep playing the damsel in distress. Do yourself a favor and live your truth. It'll be uncomfortable at times. It will hurt like hell at others. The difference between living in that truth and living where you are now is that the authenticity of those moments will feel way better than the watered down and edited version of life you currently dwell in.

Toxic Special Victim Unit - The Martyr

The Martyr is a victim with a purpose and a plan. Her intent is to make sure you know the situation she suffers from is the result of her never-ending efforts to help someone else. She is the type to tell you how much she would love to go out with you, but she doesn't have any money. Had she not splurged last night at your celebratory happy hour, she would be there right now. She will mention her financial woes to ensure you remember she covered your drinks that night. Not that she blames you, of course. But had you only drunk one cocktail instead of three, she might be on your doorstep now. She will remind you how she covered parking, and left a hefty tip, all of which leaves her completely penniless now.

She won't remember how you said you didn't want to go in the first place. How she insisted as her treat. Or how she had four drinks herself. Noooooo, she is too busy keeping tabs on the spinach artichoke dip appetizer you split. The exact one you wish you could regurgitate right now and give back to her to shut her up.

She gives constantly to any and everyone. That seems so admirable and impressive, but it is a load of bull. She is not sacrificing out of the goodness of her heart. She is making sure she does enough good deeds to keep those around her in her debt. This tit-for-tat-style list of friendly accomplishments is draining. Do you owe her? Does she owe you? Are you really her friend, or just a beneficiary to her constant gifts? Should you borrow the twenty dollars you really need today in exchange for the forty minutes of her mentioning it later? Or ride out on your gas light and a prayer? AAA is a better back up than her anyway.

Party Pooper

Amanda's friend Danielle recently offered to help prepare for a birthday party Amanda was hosting for a mutual friend. Amanda knew Danielle tended to do too much and then remind you of that fact shortly after, so she declined her help. Although the event was an effort amongst their group, she just knew it was not worth the extra drama.

As the date for the party approached, Amanda realized there were some time-sensitive things that she would not be able to complete herself. One of them was on Danielle's side of town. First, she asked her other friends if they could step in. Of course they couldn't, that would have been too perfect.

She weighed her options. She could go without said items or ask Danielle to help. She knew Danielle would eagerly assist. She was probably sitting by the phone now, waiting with bated breath, hoping she could come in and save the day. It irked Amanda to her core that she would have to give her that satisfaction, but she had no choice. She couldn't sacrifice the quality of the party because Danielle "might" have something to say.

She sent the SOS. Danielle, as expected, said she could help. Amanda asked if there was anything that would make this an undue hardship. Danielle assured her it would be no problem. Amanda swallowed her doubt, thanked Danielle for her help, and proceeded to complete other tasks for the day.

As prep began for the party begins, Danielle arrives with the requested items, but in clearly no condition to stay. It is a themed party and she is not dressed for the occasion. Soon, everyone starts to ask why she's not dressed. She tells them how getting the items took more time than anticipated and she didn't have time to retrieve her outfit. Rather than be late with the stuff, she rushed over here to make sure the party had what it needed. She then offers to go back home to get her outfit. But if she does, she will certainly be late returning and will waste her much needed gas. Since she is between pay periods, she doesn't think it is a good idea to make two trips, so, she is just going to stay home.

Amanda could not have wanted to punch Danielle or herself more than in that moment. She knew Danielle's help would cost her more than it was worth. Everyone urged a "reluctant" Danielle to stay even though she was not in theme. Especially because she went so far out of her way to get things. Amanda, along with a few other women who were up to speed on Danielle's typical shenanigans, knew that was probably her goal in the first place and just tried to avoid her for the duration of the party. Still, they could not help but overhear her repeated recount of her ordeal to different guests, explaining why she was not dressed properly. There was not one attendee who did not know her personal sacrifice for the night's festivities. Danielle sucked up the extra attention and adoration the way Amanda knew she would.

How to Deal with a Martyr

Don't let her do anything for you. If she suggests, decline. If she offers, decline. If she insists, decline. Be like a maxed-out credit card: decline, decline, decline! She will have to get her giving kicks from someone else. I do not care how much you need the help, all money ain't good money. Her input is tainted. It comes at a cost way higher than what you are receiving. Short and simple. You don't want what she has; you want who she is. Especially with a Martyr, the only way to ensure she knows that is to only accept friendship from her. Nothing else.

Dear Martyrs,

Putting someone else's wellbeing before yours is the epitome of being a good friend. Sacrifice is not only admirable but is often essential. I commend you. You deserve accolades, applause and awards. Oh, maybe a statue? No! A monument will be the only thing that will suffice in shutting you up about all you do. You know, a considerate act loses much of its appeal when it must be acknowledged over and over and over again. It appears you are not doing all these acts for the sake of being gracious, but because you want the whole world to know exactly how gracious you can be.

We get it. Congratulations! Now stop pointing out the knife before you dramatically throw yourself on it. Sometimes we give a lot more than what we get. Sometimes we don't get the thank you we deserve after we perform an act they didn't deserve. We all feel we are owed a pat on the back for doing what we don't necessarily want or must do. But how many pats do you need?

If the satisfaction of the act does not satisfy you, you are toxic by way of kindness. There is a reason you feel the need to not only place everyone else's needs before yourself but also consistently inform them you are doing so.

Want to know how to turn a positive into a negative in a blink of an eye? Keep being a Martyr. We want to believe our friends support us and help us just because they want to be there in our time of need. Not because they want to hold it over us in a long scorecard we can never balance. If the only way you can keep your friends around is to rein them in with unrequited favors, they just aren't that into you. I promise I will still consider you a good person if you don't point it out. You're doing the most damage to yourself. In addition to pushing your friends away, you are overextending yourself and stretching your capabilities unnecessarily. Aren't you tired yet?

THE DOUBTER

Toxic Tip: When you build a wall around yourself, you block yourself from all experiences. Good and Bad.

Her Toxic Scale: "I don't have any friends," to "Women are the spawn of the Devil."

If there is one trait that confuses me more than others, it is the Doubter. I find it hard to decide if she:

A. Believes all women but her are evil

B. Thinks we are all unworthy of her friendship

C. Is so jaded by toxic women that she won't allow herself to get close to anyone again.

D. All of the above.

If you have a friend in this category, you must be exhausted from trying to convince her that you are worthy of her friendship. You're being hyper-diligent in making sure you don't do anything that would make you one of "those" women, and it will eventually take its toll.

Can you really be one hundred percent invested in an association you have little faith in? Well, ask a Doubter. She is the woman who reminds you, often, how she does not trust women, does not have female friends, and would prefer to be alone than to deal with the drama that women bring. Just to recap, she is a woman as well, but is miraculously excluded from the rest of us in this situation. You don't need hordes of friends just to prove you believe in friendship. However, I am cautious of women who put a cap on the friendships they can participate in based off of a toxic probability percentage they have hypothesized in their heads.

The Doubter is toxic because she is too willing to think of what can go wrong within a friendship and use that as her reasoning to not participate in one. The problem is, she does have friends. Friends who feel like they're getting stabbed in the back every time she says she can trust no one. Friends who may share her same warped sense of solitude, even as she is sharing her life with them. Yep, typically, even the Doubter finds a bestie along the way.

Don't Fail Me

One of Brianna's close friends, Brooke, tells her often that she is her only friend. She has associates, but when it comes to friends, Brianna is the beginning and end of that short list. At first, Brianna was flattered. Yay! She is so awesome she could break down Brooke's walls and be the one person Brooke can be truly open with. Then it dawned on her: she didn't really break down her walls. They are still very much intact and up for everyone else. Brooke only temporarily opened the back door and let Brianna in. Now they are both closed within Brooke's very small world. Soon, Brianna starts to feel claustrophobic inside a friendship that she is terrified of ruining.

This pressure isn't just because she thinks Brooke is awesome and doesn't want to lose her friendship. It is also because Brianna is overly cognizant of the position of power she has in Brooke's future perceptions of any friendship. She must provide a positive experience.

But Brianna isn't always positive. She knows she can range from needy to distant and back again. She also knows showing toxicity around Brooke has a completely different weight than it would with someone who is more comfortable having friends.

Brooke's expectations are unobtainable. She hasn't accepted that it is impossible to have a perfect relationship with an imperfect person. Consequently, Brianna struggles to go against her opinions, correct her actions, or tell her when she is not being good friend. Brianna knew she was contributing to Brooke's unrealistic idea of a normal friendship, and it felt increasingly impossible to maintain. While this unhealthy alliance was initially rooted in Brooke's fears, it was Brianna's concern about enacting those fears that made their relationship suffer further. As much as Brianna enjoyed being friends with Brooke, she was not enjoying the weight of their combined worries. She needed to find a way to tell Brooke, friendships aren't about being afraid.

What does a Doubter do that just drives us up the wall? She informs us that she is a Doubter. *All the time!* At brunch, on the plane, at a party, on vacation, she never wants you to forget how much she isn't counting on things to work. It is hard enough to be a great friend without being reminded that if you are not, you will completely destroy her last shred of belief in female friendships. But, no pressure.

Doubters are created. She has either been raised by another Doubter to question all women or has been damaged. Remember, friendship heartbreaks are just as difficult to overcome as the romantic kind. Depending on how long ago it was, or how close they were, if the last close friend she had left her in a bad way, it will take some time before she can bounce back from that experience. Her trust was not just destroyed in that person, but in the institution of friendship itself.

The effects of a bad relationship can run deep and change someone for years after. Just like that guy you dated who told you, "I wanna get close, but I have been hurt so much in the past." The lifespan of that disappointment may surpass what you believe reasonable. For some, the healing is slow and incomplete. From those wounds, a Doubter is born. Even if she can be open and honest about her toxic doubting ways, she is toxic because her baggage will still negatively affect your friendship.

How to Deal with a Doubter

It makes sense to be hesitant about investing in someone who tells you from the beginning that they do not think you are trustworthy enough to care about. Like, why are you there? For their admittedly limited association? Don't you have enough to do in a day already? Trying to build a friendship with a Doubter seems like a lose-lose situation. However, Doubters don't really want to go through life without friends. They are just either too scared or too lazy to commit to something that isn't guaranteed. They don't want to be rebuffed or disappointed, so they pretend to be discouraged or uninterested.

Guess what! No one enjoys rejection or heartbreak, and you don't have to be a Doubter to have those fears. You don't have to be a Doubter to not want to waste your time befriending someone who is going to make you regret it later. Uncertainty is not a valid excuse to alienate an entire population of people. She gets compassion, but not a pass to be toxic.

So, what do you do when you encounter this kind of woman? Be real. Remember, doubting is the defense mechanism. She is operating based off speculative expectations of a negative situation. Don't cater to her unfounded concern. That means, show your fabulousness and your flaws. She will have to accept you as is. Do not, and I do mean do not, be faux-perfect. It is not sustainable and it is not healthy. You may as well represent yourself for who you are and what you have to offer from the beginning. If she is going to run at the first sign of your humanity, this was never going to work in the first place. You are not obliged to overcompensate for her past. What you do owe her is authenticity and transparency.

If you know that you have a hard time keeping plans, following through, or showing up, do not befriend this woman. You are making the situation worse. Doubters are a challenge because their threshold for conflict is lower than average. If you are a bit of a Drama Queen, Pessimist, or Victim, this is not the person you want to try to connect with because you will not improve her outlook on women or friendships. It is irresponsible on your part to try to engage with an incompatible personality type, knowing you will be setting the stage to transfer and absorb toxicity back and forth.

Doubters do well with women who have some patience for their reservations. For example, you need to be comfortable with being on the outskirts of her life in the beginning. If you invite her to family barbecue, that invitation may not be reciprocated right away. You must understand when she shields her feelings until she is able to relax around you. Allow the friendship to progress at her pace.

That doesn't mean that you deserve to get stepped on or feel unappreciated until she recognizes your internal awesomeness. It means that slow and steady is likely the safest speed for her. Her vetting process will be longer than yours. While you may be willing and ready to declare her your BFF two months in, that title and role may take a year for her to feel comfortable in. Doubters want friendship as much as all of us; however, they need to overcome their own strenuous risk management process to let it happen. Don't nominate yourself for that challenge if you can't handle it.

Dear Doubters,

It's astonishing how quickly you Doubters will tell me how and why you are unable to have beneficial relationships with other women. By being that raw emotionally, you're opening yourself up to the exact relationship you insist you're incapable of having. I know I have a knack for getting people to open up, but even if I had a sign on my forehead labeling me a safe zone, I still represent the exact connection you claim you want to avoid. Which leads me to conclude, you don't really want to avoid it at all, you just want to control it too much.

Stop restricting amazing. I don't know who lied to you, but all women are not out to get you. Frankly, I have never been so devastated by a friend that I thought it better to never have one again. But I do know, whoever led you astray, you're letting her continue to hinder and hurt you every time you decide to be a one-man wolf pack. Let her go. Let the pain she brought you go too. Carrying it with you wherever you go is just weighing you down. I can guarantee whoever played a role in making you a non-believer has moved on. You should do the same.

If you think you've gotten beyond it because you have accepted you're a Doubter, you haven't. Moving on isn't declaring to be forever alone. Moving on isn't pretending you can rely on no one but yourself. There is someone for everyone. There is a community of love you can participate in. You can like being alone most of the time. You can be socially awkward. You can be extremely introverted. There are plenty of women who would love to coexist with you in that occasional, weird, or quiet world. Stop playing like you don't want to join in. Stop denying you don't feel like you're missing out. Stop. So we can start being friends.

PART THREE:

OUR TOXIC WORLD

Toxic women exist beyond definition and theory. From the playground to the retired living community—outside of living in complete seclusion—there is no way to prevent coexisting with one another. It is not a matter of who or what; it is matter of when and how. They will share our homes, residencies, and break rooms. We will share secrets with them in homeroom and share power points with them at conventions.

It is easier to welcome the thought of dealing with all that differing toxicity when you feel you are prepared for it. This section is about getting ready for the world around you with a new skill set. You have already accomplished so much. You have established a commitment to better yourself. You are able to recognize and navigate through toxic traits in both yourself and the women around you. Now you must analyze the spaces you regularly occupy to ensure your new toxic life isn't derailed by your old toxic environments.

A FAMILY TRAIT

Unlike the friends you decide to no longer care to deal with, not being around a sister or cousin can prove difficult. These relationships are often seen as mandatory. The term "blood is thicker than water" exists because we have a higher set of expectations for the women in our families than for the women we meet along the way—a loyalty that cannot be broken. When these conjectures are not met, or these women prove just as toxic as anyone else, it has a completely different effect.

Being enemies with someone who has the potential to share your space on a regular basis, interact with people you know all the time, or have the seat across from you come Christmas Day is more than just a run-in with an ex-Bestie. You wouldn't even approach that type of confrontation the same way. As a staple in our diet of relationships, your families are crucial for maintaining a healthy level of toxicity in your life, ideally by providing consolation and comfort from the outside toxic world. In reality, few have not had a toxic relationship with a woman from within the familial fold. This goes beyond fighting over toys when we are tots. I have seen enough episodes of *Maury* to know that a Ken doll can turn into a man a decade later and tear close women apart.

To add fuel to this fire, your discontent can cause issues in your other relationships. Is your Dad picking your sister's side? Did your cousin choose to give support to your Auntie over you? You can understand that she is her Mom, but right is still right, and wrong, well, is her Mom. Does the spectator's indifference infuriate you more than if they stood against you? You deal with the anger, disappointment, and looming guilt over not being able to forgive and forget in the most intimate space possible: your home.

It is important to be aware that family doesn't equal perfect and it never equals non-toxic. You have options. Family designation doesn't mean we have to passively accept their toxic behavior; you possess the power of deciding how to deal with them.

Inheritance

During a successful wine night, my best friend and I were discussing the relationships between mothers, or matriarchs, and daughters. From this conversation we established that Forrest's mom was all wrong. Life isn't like a box of chocolates. I know exactly what I'm getting in my nuts and chews box from See's. Instead of those chocolates, life is like a bowl of soup.

What you are given from your mother is your stock to start with. It does not solely determine what you will become, but it develops the initial flavors of the person you are. My mother told me about her relationships and friendships of past and present. She also insisted that I have self-confidence and conviction of my worth. While she could not always understand or relate to my feelings, she attempted to remain connected to me throughout our hardships. She gave me all she had to start me off with the best of herself.

This is my stock. It is rich with the salty tears of her failures and smooth with her triumph. It is dense with complexity from her relationships with her own mother and sister, spicy from her fighter spirit, and satisfyingly truthful to the soul. Conversely my friend feels as though she has been given slightly less in her stock. She was given the same sweetness of love as I was, but her stock lacks the depth of character. Her mother is more reserved than my own. She has maintained a secrecy of history that leaves my friend wondering, "Who do I come from? What am I made of?"

Some people are given such rich stock that they have little left to add to feel complete. A few vegetables, maybe a nice cut of meat, and they have a flavorful and enriching soup for their soul. Others are not as fortunate. They are given little to nothing to begin their development. Instead of broth, they are given water. They must literally put their bones into making themselves from scratch. That does not mean that they will not eventually end up with a great flavor. Their soup could be even better than someone else's who was given more; they just have to put more ingredients into their effort.

Your recipe is never complete. You are never too old to change the contents of yourself. Always continue to stew and develop your own greatness. Worst case scenario, start over completely from scratch, and build yourself up all over again.

Pay It Forward

When raising little women, be sure to consider what you are contributing to their stock. It is a privilege to have the opportunity to share with and mold another person. I consider my young nieces my best friends for a reason. It is not just that they are fun to color with and allow me to constantly relive my childhood through our adventures—however, great that bonus. I continuously call them my best friends because I want them to have a strong foundation for what they should have in a friendship. I want to contribute the best of myself to their stock.

Setting the qualifications for a healthy friendship will empower them earlier and leave them less likely to be involved in toxic relationships later. If I love and respect them, show them attention, and continue to be there for them, they will associate that with not just an Auntie does, but what best friends do. Support your little women and allow them to support you. Actively participate in their lives and allow them to exercise their friendship muscles by mimicking you. It is never too early to build them up and set the definition for what friendship is.

We should also strive to serve as an example to the younger girls and women in our communities through our adult relationships. If they see their female role models constantly arguing with the women in their family, they will believe that behavior is acceptable. Just like if they see you putting down women on TV or at the grocery store, they will do the same. Negative behavior is learned; therefore, be mindful what you say about those who are *not* your friends as well. Why go out of your way to teach tolerance of race, religion, socio-economic status, or appearance and not make an active effort to extend that umbrella of compassion to cover women without exception?

Raise friend geniuses. Nurture young women with the fortitude to stand on their own and the ability to feel comfortable within a group of their peers. It is essential to cultivate social skills as much as any subject taught in school. My nieces, my best friends, may be president one day, or they can just be amazingly non-toxic women. Either way, they can use the relationship skills they are learning now to advance beyond any toxic situation they will inevitably come across.

Ensure a better world for every woman you know, including yourself, by grooming the little women in your world. Their emotional development will shape their existence as much as any other facet of their life; do not let them down.

You Want Too Much

Family is typically the first line of your support system. Your instant babysitters, therapists, and occasional ATMs can all live under your roof. Having these resources at hand can solve problems with ease, or they can easily create more problems. What is family for if not to bend to your every whim and supply everything that you are lacking? Wait. That was the toxic switch. That is the phrase you don't say out loud, but that is how you act.

This is the easiest group of women to underrate and overrun. There is such a grand idea of what family demands, you forget that every Friday your niece may not enjoy tutoring her cousins for free. You forget that your unemployed sister may not have a job, but she sure didn't get hired as your live-in au pair. You forget that your mom might want to spend her savings on herself instead of making up the balance you owe in rent... every single month. You forget the thank yous and the hugs of appreciation because your expectations have surpassed reason.

You cannot go out of our way to keep your friends satisfied and feeling appreciated but neglect to give that same attention to the women with whom you share DNA. I do not know how we have managed to allow the ratio between what we give and receive get so lopsided, but if we do not equalize the balance between our assumptions and obligations, we will end up with a relationship, and a family, that is nothing but toxic. Make sure the women in your family feel valued for who they are and what they do for you.

Compare and Contrast

A little competition within the family is typically seen as a great motivator. If your sister makes the varsity cheerleading squad in 11th grade, you want to make it in 10th grade. If your mother was chapter president, it only makes sense that you will be too. However, it is not uncommon that the friendly fight turns into a full-blown war filled with not so friendly fire. And it is completely toxic.

Family rivalry gone wrong can lead to a contention that destroys any chance of a loving relationship. Struggling to match up to those around you can lead to self-esteem deficiencies and animosity directed toward the woman who is considered successful. These potential toxic hazards are just as exacerbating if she finds joy in reveling in her achievements to put you down than if she is shown favoritism because of her accomplishments. It is hard to feel happy for someone else, family or not, if their joy is directly linked to your sorrow.

The labels like the smart one, the pretty one, or the cool one can define what your role is inside and outside of the home. What ends up happening if the best parts of you aren't easily categorized? You risk losing your self-worth in everyone else's definitions. You fight yourself to fit in, or fight everyone else so that they include you. When trying to out-unique each other, you only negate the things that bind you and force unnecessary separation.

For those who are in positions to exacerbate these comparisons or demand these differences between the women in their family, recognize that there is a limit to healthy competition. If you push your loved ones beyond this level, you are introducing conflict, with toxicity as the only outcome. Do not create needless division under the guise of pushing them to their best. If your true intent is for everyone to reach their personal potential, highlight and celebrate everyone's individuality equally. In the instances when interests overlap, compliment the best in everyone involved.

Everyone does not have the same capability for a reason. Don't lose sight of that. Sisters, cousins, mothers, and daughters should not categorize one another as adversaries. It voids the beauty of those intimate relationships to replace them with the dog-eat-dog world that is already waiting for them as soon as they walk out the door. Maintain the solace of home by creating and keeping it a safe space.

Exit Strategy

Would you leave a pot of water to simmer forever on the back burner of the stove? No. Because even if it never boils over, you must continually pour water into that pot to make sure that once it burns out, the pot itself isn't ruined. Do yourself a favor and take the pot off the stove completely. Save yourself the effort of trying to keep it to a simmer and just dump the water, the negative association, and the problem.

We have an obligation to our personal health that may require separation from certain women in our family despite the blood we share. If she is toxic, she is toxic. There is no equation that deducts toxicity points depending on what relation she has to us. As I have mentioned, it makes the decision more difficult, but it is still your decision. We cannot view limitation or removal of a toxic family member as a betrayal against our bloodline. That narrow view of our options will restrict us into continuing terrible relationships with women just because we are related. We deserve peace and serenity in our lives, period. If we cannot achieve that and talk to our extremely judgmental grandma daily, well, Memaw needs to be contacted less often.

We owe our family respect, and in turn they owe us the same. There is no law that states respecting one another cannot include respecting the space and boundaries that you establish. Don't make yourself a Victim or Phony for the sake of saving face. Family or foe, when it is no longer a safe situation for your wellbeing, you need to choose yourself. Self-preservation is the determination that you matter more than anything else. It is not the right to disregard other people as insignificant, but rather the opportunity to recognize the significance in yourself.

If you do feel the need to make an emotional separation from a family member, attempt to discuss it with them first. Remember, even when it is uncomfortable, tell the person on the other side of the threshold why you are closing the door before you slam it in their face. They need to know why you are away, not just that you are gone. Escapism is not a healthy way to handle conflict with our friends or families.

If you never address with the problem between you, it leaves a space for those issues to continue and spread to other family members. If the understanding on both sides is mutual, other family members will feel less obligated to pick sides, provide buffers, or play referee when things get heated. You don't want to jeopardize your relationship with another person because you didn't control this one. You need to be able to share family members without resentment and jealousy. You need to be able to share space without making other people uncomfortable. There will be women you love as family whom you will never like as friends. It is okay as long as you are okay about it.

Mommy Dearest

What about my mama?! She birthed me. She raised me. She is my mama! Yes, this includes the potential separation from your own mother. Her story about your prolonged labor ruining her vagina does not make her safe. I know this is a frightful position to be in. For a select few, the most toxic relationship they will ever have is the one with their own mother. They too deserve a way out.

Everything in life tells you that you should not be at odds with your mother. Biology connects you on the most primal level. But life happens. Life happened to your mother before you were born. Life happened to her afterward and is still happening to her now. Oddly, it's almost as though you are not programmed to see your mother as a woman, just as your mom. Your mother is a woman with history and dreams. It is essential to recognize the humanity in our mothers in order to accept their limitations. She cannot and will not be perfect.

Sadly, she may be the most toxic person that you ever encounter. She has the capability to hurt you as much as anyone else you know. These are realities we have to acknowledge and deal with.

I assure you that although she gave you life and you are intrinsically pre-disposed to absorb her toxicity, you do not have to. You do not have to remain in an abusive relationship because she birthed you and raised you or because she is your mama. You owe it to yourself, and ironically even to the mother who is making it difficult, to live your best life. You cannot accomplish that by absorbing the worst of her.

Love, tradition, heritage, guilt, and coercion can make any an emotional barrier between yourself and your mother seem disrespectful or even traitorous. When we see a friend or family member accepting toxic behavior from their mother, we understand why she accepts those sub-par conditions for their relationship. We are not regularly reminded that we have the choice of compliance. We do. You do. In every relationship, including this one.

You do not have to be disrespected or belittled. You do not have to compensate for your mother's toxic shortcomings. You do not have to sacrifice your joy, your goals, or your freedom. You do not have to suffer for the sake of your mother's love. If your complete submission, regardless of the detriment it brings you, is the only way to secure your mother's love and contentment with your relationship, you may want to consider if it is a relationship you can fully participate in.

It is unreasonable to expect your daughter to carry the brunt of responsibility in the upkeep of your relationship by remaining subservient. Extended submission within any relationship will lead to a noxious environment. If the subjugation of your daughter is the only dynamic of the relationship that maintains its existence, it is a toxic relationship.

This is a controversial and taboo subject, but yes, at some point in life, you should be your mother's equal. Kinda. The dynamics of your relationship should change and transition through time to allow for mutual respect to happen. If you as a mother believe your daughter should heel to you for the sole reason that you raised her, you may want to remind yourself that her existence is based solely on your decision to have her. You chose her; she did not choose you. Your relationship needs to progress beyond forced adherence, so you become her choice as well.

I love and respect my mother. While she has always loved me, she now also respects me as woman. That means she listens to my thoughts and opinions without dismissal based on hierarchy. That means she asks and does not just demand. That means she thanks and does not just expect. I can say no and maintain being respectful and she can now hear "no" and not immediately feel impudence. These are aspects that you can seek in your relationship with your mother. In fact, if these abilities are not already reflected in your relationship with you mother, you should work towards them. Don't be afraid to ask for more. Your relationship with your mothers should become comfortable for you both. Don't limit the potential greatness based off antiquated conditions of docility.

As much as control and dominance can be gratifying in a one-dimensional way, it cannot lead to anything but unhealthy hostility later on. This goes for older sisters, cousins, aunties, and grandmothers as well. If you let your title decide the temperament of your relationship, you will at best have dissatisfaction and at worst distance to prevent future interaction. You have a choice. You can share your relationship and actually have one, or you can dictate and lose out on shared gratification.

This is not an open invitation for my teenage readers to inform their mothers that their unwillingness to allow them to stay out until the wee hours of the morning has created an uncomfortable relationship. Nah, Boo Boo, that is not what I'm saying. This is a reassurance that you can grow into having a better sense of connection based on more than "because I said so," if both parties are willing to work for it.

It also means if you want your relationship to progress, you also cannot rest on your title to seek and demand more from your mom than is reasonable. That means you cannot be twenty-four years old making your own decisions and also expect your mother to live her life based off those decisions. If you decide to go on a different path than the one your mother imagined, she should support that, but she is not required to walk it with you. Respect does not always equate agreement. She does not owe you her stamp of approval; she owes you her unconditional love. Do not confuse the two.

You may always be her child, but if you want to seen and treated with the respect of an adult, you must grow beyond your childish ways. Unless you're sick. Then you get a pass, because every sick child needs to be coddled a little, regardless of age.

In addition to monitoring our toxic behavior, we need to be not just sisters, moms, aunts, and cousins, but also good friends. We have to stop taking our relatives for granted. We cannot expect all the benefits of family ties without giving the wonderful women who surround us the friendship they deserve. We do our relative relationships a disservice when we assume that *family* and *friend* are synonymous and do not dedicate enough effort to maintaining positive associations. Invest in your family relationships, and take advantage of the complete benefits of being a loved one.

#SOCIALMEDIASINS

Social media has transformed communication. From commerce and outreach to propaganda and promposals, there is nothing we cannot access or achieve through our phones and laptops. We can build businesses, share our greatest accomplishments, and get advice and pho recipes without pulling out our Rolodex or dusty encyclopedias. I can have three simultaneous conversations going with my friend through text, Facebook, and Instagram, each with its own subject and tone, throughout the week. It is the new way of life, and our relationships must adapt to survive the new climate. Some of us will fight tooth and nail to never fully integrate it into our personal lives; others of us have had it seamlessly intertwine with how we interact. However infrequently or abundantly it's used, we need to ensure that we are curating and keeping our online life a healthy space for our relationships to thrive.

Confession: I like watching people be messy. I am slightly envious of their apparent disregard for privacy or decency. I wish I had that freedom to say, "Screw it all! I am going to be uncensored to the detriment of my reputation!" Although I try to remove drama from my life, a friend on social media will provide a dose of foolishness and remind me that others are not so active in their own efforts. I then become a willing spectator to other women dealing with their toxicity in a public forum. It's hard not to. The question then becomes how much toxicity you can observe before it turns into actions that you internalize and emulate.

Denying that your electronic activity and engagement contributes directly to your toxic journey can only leave you with a hazardous blind spot. You must assess your virtual presence with the same care as you do your physical interactions. There are plenty of things you should stop doing online: sending chain messages, reposting from fake celebrity accounts promising fortunes, and taking a posed photo and then captioning it "candid." Those things are annoying, but they aren't harmful. There are more important mistakes you're making that are increasing your toxic footprint—actions you should red-light and stop.

Stop the 7 Social Media Sins

1. Stop Enabling

Since some women use their social media as open diaries, you are forced to decide whether to join along on their toxic ride or banish them to the poisonous wasteland. This will require you to unfriend and unfollow people you may not want to, but need to. Maintaining healthy levels on your toximeter is hard enough without allotting valuable reserves on OPP: other people's problems.

What do you do if a friend keeps crying to the world on the internet even though you've offered her a shoulder to do that exact thing? Ignore it. Do not comment on the status to ask additional clarifying questions. You're enabling her to continue to use an unhealthy platform for addressing issues. There is a difference between crying out for help and crying out for attention.

Not everyone who is her "friend" on Facebook has her best interest at heart. Refrain from requesting private information in a public forum. If you want to remind her that you are there for her, call her or text her. A simple inquiry into her general wellbeing gives her the opportunity to address whatever she has going on. You do not have to acknowledge that you know via the internet of any issues she may be having. If she wants to vent and discuss her problems, she will take you up on your offer. Now, if this is a consistent trend and she never utilizes you as a resource for support, you may have to re-evaluate your role in the relationship. She may have no interest in receiving actual help and just be seeking attention for the sake of validation. That is toxic, and you want no part of it.

2. Stop Following

Don't follow people on social media who annoy you. Why? Because everything that they post will annoy you. They post a cute baby picture... annoying. They saved a cat from a fire... super annoying. Oh! A Noble Peace Prize... how annoying can you be?! For some reason, women follow other women just to say something negative in their comments. There are women who want to know every move another woman makes, just to have the opportunity to criticize or condemn her. Who has the time to worry about people they do not like and be delusional enough to believe that their opinion about those people matter? Not only is that a double dose of dumb, that is toxic behavior at its finest.

If you are one of these poor misguided women, PLEASE STOP! You're embarrassing yourself. As much as I try to rationalize most toxic behaviors, this is another instance in which I must draw the line. If you are actively following the actions of another woman, just to remind yourself you do not like her or anything that she does, you need to do some soul searching and return to your logical self. You can try to convince yourself you are only looking at what they put out into the world, but that still doesn't explain your need see it. If you have already established that she is someone you are not fond of, why are you volunteering your viewership? Use your energy for a greater purpose. In fact, since you are so good on the world wide web, maybe you can enlist the services of your GPS to locate the good sense you've lost.

3. Stop Thinking That You're Helping

There is a reason celebrities are constantly in the limelight now. It's not for their talents in their profession, but for the things they allow the public to know. These women are just as toxic as the rest of us, and struggling to find healthy ways to work through grievances that don't include being messy in 280 characters. Their toxicity is now open for the world to see, critique, and absorb.

When observing rifts between celebrities on social media, what I notice even more than the bitter battle between the stars is the embroiled discourse between their fans and foes alike. They are eager to soak up anything their idol gives them. Whether a photo, movie, album, fashion line, or toxic tirade, it will be consumed with fervor. The issue with being associated with someone, even a celebrity, is you become invested. Many people have difficulty separating their personal connection with that entertainer and the reality that there is no personal connection to that entertainer.

Don't be misled to believe that if you are "defending" your favorite that you are not also toxic. While your heart may be in a decent place, your actions are a waste. Don't spend precious energy engaging in dialogue with someone whose sole purpose is to be the negative to your positive. More so, no matter how witty a response or scathing a rebuttal, in the end you lost the most important thing you have: your time. That woman you were fighting still doesn't like you or that celebrity and will come back tomorrow to do the same thing. Are you so invested in being right about a matter that is completely subjective that you are willing to sacrifice the one thing that you will never get back?

3.5. Stop Arguing with Internet Trolls

This extends beyond celebrity. This applies everything from the mommy blogs to the political pages. Stop using the comment section to exercise your toxic muscles. Who is more the fool, the person spewing toxic things or the one responding to them? You are entitled to your opinion and you are also entitled to express it. Those same entitlements are given to everyone else who has a login. Some use them to encourage dialogue, and many use them to encourage toxicity. There is a difference. Always ensure you are the former and not the latter.

There are too many women who use the act of arguing to fulfill some unfortunate void within themselves. Those women need a hug, not a platform to display their toxic behavior like a proud peacock. These trolls are looking for a response. If they are ignored, they have no chance to continue to respond, and they aren't succeeding in pulling out desired responses in other women. Let their negativity stay with them. Without your input, they will have to find other means to entertain themselves. Comments are rarely used as a space to engage in progressive conversation. Quickly things go from factual, to figurative, to personal. Never get personal with a stranger online. They do not know you. You do not know them. Why are you fighting them? What do you plan on achieving? Scroll away, every single time.

4. Stop Misusing Your Influence

The correlation between followers and finances is a slippery slope. Suddenly being an influencer includes more than just giving your opinion on the latest offering from the cosmetic counter. Influencing is now an opportunity for brands to compensate you for being the face of their product. With so many women amassing thousand—and millions—of followers, their audience becomes the prime location to boost sales... and toxicity.

If you are one of these women, it is imperative you maintain your integrity. I am not here to count anyone else's coins or prevent any woman from capitalizing on her popularity to make money, but be mindful of not just what you are selling, but who you are selling it to, as well as the effect it can have on that demographic. We have discussed the importance of advertising authentically and not just seeing your social media presence as an opportunity to come up, but this is the moment to really think about your impact.

It is just as crucial to monitor what you do, post, and participate in, beyond what you are trying to sell, to ensure it is healthy. Power can be addicting. The knowledge that what you wear, support, or even mention can reach women you will never meet can become an obsession. Make sure your influence is positive. If you are having a toxic moment or thought, it is not something you need to spread to your followers. Especially if you utilize your social media presence as a business more than as a refection of your personal life, be cognizant of how you are representing yourself; the health of those who are subscribing and watching depends on it.

5. Stop Being a Bully

Do not create a separate set of rules for yourself or others when online. Always remember who you are outside of your screen name. That is person you should try to be in all situations and relationships, regardless of the medium of communication. If you are suddenly bolder, braver, or bitchier, understand that you cannot restrict that person to online; you *are* that person. Enacting these traits through the internet does not reduce your ownership of the actions or their repercussions. If feel so strong and empowered to go full toxic only when you are safely behind the protection of the web, you're not only toxic you're a ~~wuss~~, ~~punk~~, jackass.

I don't know why niceties fly out of the html portal. But there ya'll are, acting a whole ass online, and thinking it is okay. Treat other women with respect and consideration. If you are starting any post with "I'm sorry but..." just delete the whole thing. You aren't sorry and you're definitely about to say something out of line. Ask yourself, why? Why do you feel your rudeness is covered under opinion? It isn't. Neither is your racism, classism, ignorance, or xenophobia. Nothing is going to be forgiven because you typed it instead of said it.

You are free to be whomever you want, but you cannot disengage from that when you log off. If you think otherwise, think about the many people who have had their lives altered by words they have typed on social media. Their scholarships, occupations, reputations, and futures—all gone. They tearfully attempt to reconcile their horrid words online with their kindness offline. Ultimately, they are judged and destroyed by their chosen depiction of themselves. Don't switch up and get caught up.

6. Stop Oversharing

Do not share anything online that you are not prepared to defend. The internet can be a toxic place, depending on the amount of access you give others to view and comment on your personal life. The wide net of accessibility leaves us exposed to friends, foes, and strangers. A simple post of a picture can be analyzed and criticized relentlessly. An error in a tweet can be retweeted and then mocked. Personal moments can become memes, and suddenly you are the face of the next viral trend. If you are unprepared for those possibilities, do not post.

We are always advised that we should assume anything we share on any platform is open for the world to view. Even with the strictest privacy settings, your pictures, words, and concepts can be shared and scrutinized instantly. If you are uncomfortable with that, limit what you share. Save your most intimate moments, the parts of yourself you want private, off the internet.

I know it is hard to imagine, but a great age of human interaction occurred without ever pressing send. I enjoy social media as much as the next person, but the internet will never get the full story. I save the best for those who mean the most in my life. Invest in your friendships outside of social media, and you will not be so dependent on these interactions to validate their importance. Selective sharing is your best defense to social media toxicity and your greatest opportunity to curate healthy relationships.

7. Stop Playing Make-Believe

Just like you should not overshare, you should not play pretend. If you are using social media as an opportunity to portray the life you want instead of the one you have, you may want to figure out a few whys. Why do you feel your life isn't good enough, and why do you need to share at all? You do not have to live feed your entire day to verify authenticity; just don't go out of your way to lie.

If my car is dirty, I'm not going to post it. But I am also not going to post an old picture of my car with the caption "freshly washed." There is a big difference between omitting what you consider embarrassing or unworthy of sharing and lying to keep up the facade of a life that doesn't exist. Don't post "wheels up" with a picture of someone else's passport. Don't post a picture of you and your boo with the caption "my always and forever" if you are one day away from a breakup.

Sometimes life happens to us, and the results aren't what we want. It is okay to go through those moments privately. It is even more okay to go through those moments and not try to overcompensate for them by pretending they are not happening. You may shrug this all off, as it is just social media, but who are you trying to convince, impress, or entertain with the lies you spread on *just* social media? Let the truth set you free. Let it keep you from not accepting your reality and feeling the need to create a new one online. A lie is a lie, no matter how it is told.

Inexplicably, there is a weaker definition of permittable friendship behaviors on the internet. This watered-down definition is further destroyed by women who continue to redefine and modify it at will. The lines between friends and enemies is blurred, and it is seen as acceptable to go back and forth between the two more fluidly than we would in our physical lives. It is a lot easier to be hurtful when you don't have to see the pain in someone's face, or hear the despair in their tone. Technology has become a buffer as much as it serves as a connector, and we need to control how utilize the benefits of both.

As time progresses and traditional communication methods die— sorry house phone—it may feel like if you are not connected through your app, you are not associated at all. This is not a condemnation of social media-based friendships. I have friends I connected with through social media, that I have never, and may never, actually meet. The mode of communication does not limit the quality of our relationship; how we participate does. When you stop doing the seven things listed in the previous pages, see what connections remain. Online or not, those are the women you have a healthy investment in.

DOLLARS AND SENSE

You work because you enjoy eating, talking on your cell phone, having a roof over your head, and having enough disposable income to buy books for leisure. I don't know why life was set up this way, but it is a finite truth that we have mostly accepted. The interesting thing about the work environment is the massive amount of time you spend around other people you did not volunteer to be around. If you are not the hiring manager, or her BFF, chances are you will have to coexist with women you may despise. When you find yourself loathing the thought of going into work, and not for the usual reasons like you could be on the beach instead, you may want to determine whether you're working in a toxic environment.

Akin to any group setting, the difficulty with maneuvering within your occupation is the wide range of personalities that you can encounter. That means you must have multiple techniques at your disposal to utilize at a moment's notice, in order to dodge, derail, and deter unwanted toxins so they don't affect you.

There are three rules to use within the workplace that will make you the least toxic person clocking in and out. Now, notice I did not say you will have a toxic-free environment. Your goal is always to control yourself and manage your surroundings. Managing does not by any means guarantee perfection. For the people and events that you cannot alter, you must regulate your reactions to them. No magic here, but another chance to improve your life through concerted effort.

The Three Rules

The Golden Rule

Simply, the Golden Rule is to always aim for a positive exchange. It is that easy. To achieve this, your goal should always be that you cannot be out-niced at work. This is a non-negotiable. There is no leeway or exception. You are paid to do a job. No one is signing your check depending on how you felt that day. To assume that business dealings, production, efficiency, or progress should somehow be dependent on your emotions is absurd. So, when you are on company time, acknowledge that you are there as an employee, and that employment is contingent on your ability to control yourself.

If you know there is a person who rubs you the wrong way for whatever reason, and that the mere sight of them makes you want to fly into a Hulk rage, avoid them. Realistically, even as we progress into our best selves, there will always be people who can get a rise out of us. Avoidance may be as positive as it can get. In those cases, if that is an option, take advantage of it. Do not feel obligated to challenge yourself to rise above every toxic situation.

In the event you cannot avoid them, be cordial. *All the time.*

Don't roll your eyes.

I am fully aware of how trying coworkers can be. However, if you react with negativity, you will look bad every single time. It is never permissible to get too personal in a professional setting. If you need to repeat it to yourself as you are parking, in the elevator, and while you review your first task for the day, do so. Never be out-niced at work. I repeat, never be out-niced at work.

Think about it. Whoever is grinding your gears has already made it easy for you to look like the better person. If those around you also see that person as a nuisance, or you did display your emotions prior to your toxic evolution, people will immediately observe and appreciate your newfound approach. They will applaud your ability to remain considerate of the workplace. Imagine, the perception of you could be transformed just by being able to say "good morning" every day.

You may work with women who ignore greetings and small talk. The kind of women you can smile at, and they grimace in return. They are so toxic they can't muster up the decency to return a "How are you?" The irrational portion of your mind will tell you to either drag them face-first down cubicle row or stop extending pleasantries. Do not allow their poor decisions change your goal of a positive exchange. Unbeknownst to you, your coworkers, supervisors, managers, or directors could be observing and noting your optimal professionalism.

The Silver Rule

The most toxic people in the workplace may not be intentionally rude or hurtful. The woman who often brings the most toxicity into her environment is the one who just does not know when to stop gifting her coworkers with her unsolicited thoughts. Whether a joke, an opinion, or criticism, she cannot contain it to just herself. She inspires The Silver Rule: Try not to piss anyone off or to hurt anyone's feelings.

At any given moment, there are a lot of controversial subjects to discuss. Most them are not work appropriate. Your job is not the place to debate the intricacies of LGBTQ legislation. It is not the place to delve into what politician you are voting for and why. You should not be holding town halls at your desk about the prison industrial complex. Have these conversations in a safe space, away from where you make your money.

I can hear you asking, "Well what can we talk about then?" Before you start incorrectly throwing around facts about your freedom of speech, guess what? It doesn't matter if your thesis on "Immigration and Assimilation of the American Dream" has been printed in *The New York Times*. Unless your occupation includes moderating discussions on said thesis, stick to your job description. One more time for the ladies who walked in late to the morning meeting: You do not get paid for your personal opinions. You get paid for your work. Stay out of your feelings and stay on task.

Take yourself out of the equation and, from a business perspective, look at why it is not in the best interest of the work environment to have select women making others uncomfortable. No one wants to waste valuable company time calling you, and the woman who reported you to HR, into the office to discuss work dynamics. Even if you understand, agree, or accept that someone has differing thoughts than you for anything that is not work related, it should be addressed any time, any place, other than at work.

Now if you are having a conversation with a coworker who is also your friend, and your relationship allows for that kind of discourse, then you are more than welcome to engage in that type of conversation with that one woman. Still, be aware that although you may not be talking to others directly, if they are in earshot of you during that conversation and decide to be offended, you are still liable for the ramifications that may occur. To avoid any issue, refrain from having unnecessarily divisive conversations in mixed company. Don't mess with your money trying to prove a point.

Avoiding toxicity also means that if someone else is creating a work environment for you that is volatile or uncomfortable, report it. I know, "snitches get stitches," but you deserve peace while you are working. You have as much right to occupy that space with comfort as everyone else. Hold the people who talk reckless accountable by documenting and reporting them, if necessary. You don't owe anyone at work a pass to harass you, directly or indirectly. When someone makes your space toxic, check her, through the proper channels of course.

The Bronze Rule

The last of the three work rules deals with work-life balance. So many women never mentally clock out of work. If not regarding actual tasks they have left, it is a coworker who is giving them grief, or the anticipation of the coworker's return. The Bronze Rule is: Leave work at work. Do not take it home with you. They don't pay you overtime for thinking about work, so stop laboring for free.

Because of deadlines, coworkers, and productivity expectations, work pressure can extend well beyond your eight hours. Remember, you are only required to perform business standards while you are there. Don't tell me you want to use your free time away from work running through the same issues you do while you're there. You still deserve to be happy at some point during your day. Leave work where it belongs.

I know there are a lot of people who work from home or own their own business. For you, separating work life and home life may be more difficult. Those two lives are so intertwined, you check your Facebook feed for business and yourself at the same time. You breathe life in your job with every exhale. The kinds of hours you dedicate to your craft are proof of those motivation slogans that come up in a Google search. For you, there may be no real way to accomplish the Bronze Rule. The upside is that you have the most control over your work environment. You don't have as many Golden and Silver Rule issues.

For you, the challenge will be defining your work schedule, so you do have a moment to exist outside of your job.

If this structure cannot occur daily because of the dynamic of your occupation or your position, make sure that you compensate by taking vacations, stay-cations, or any other kind of getaway. Go where you are not accessible 24/7 and you remember to participate in the life that you are working so hard for. Make yourself an important piece of equipment for your business. Get that mani-pedi and put your phone down. Listen to your favorite band and take a walk. Sleep. There are so many self-care things you, above any of the other working woman, need to do. Believe in the empire, the brand, or the business you are trying to build, but don't forget that the woman behind it still needs to have the strength to keep bossing up. If you find you cannot achieve separation, strive for balance.

Expensive Friends

Best case scenario: You go to work, hit it off with some awesome coworkers, and end up having some legit office besties. You hang out at work, you have occasional happy hours, and you exist in one another's lives outside of the business. This is great for so many reasons. One, it makes work a lot better when you have someone to vent to during office hours. Quietly of course, but it literally pays to vent on the company's dime. Two, work friends start to supplement your dwindling social life. It can get difficult to juggle an active social life once you factor in work, commute, school, and home commitments. Grabbing that early dinner right after work or going to the gym with a coworker while letting traffic die down can give you key moments to have a good time during the week. Lunch isn't then just an hour to eat, nap, and stare at your phone. It's a whole hour to talk, laugh, and share with your work bestie.

But be warned: The further your relationship extends outside of the office, the more complicated things can become. When choosing a work boo, you must be selective. B.E. Selective. Everyone you get along with at work does not need to come over your house. Some of your absolute favorite work BFFs should be limited to nine-to-five. It doesn't mean they're any less important to you than the ones you see outside of work. It means the quality of your friendship will not benefit from any additional interaction. That is completely okay. You may only have very similar work styles and attitudes that promote camaraderie through mutual respect. Just because you take her to lunch doesn't mean you have to take her to dinner as well.

Every relationship, even when it is a good one, will not follow the same trajectory. The best way to gauge whether you want to increase your investment and openness in a coworker friendship is to take it slow. Progress in stages. If you are at orientation with a phenomenal lady who is bomb beyond reason, although you may want to lock in best friend status a.s.a.p., remember most people are different at work than they are in the real world. The woman you are vibing with may shock you when she sheds the business attire.

Test the friendship in various ways before you claim her as a friend and start to share your outside life with her. Hang out on breaks or lunches first. Observe how she treats other women within the workplace. If she is a lone wolf, and has been one, do some research as to why. Whether she has other work friends isn't an automatic deal breaker by any means; however, if she has a slew of work enemies, that is a red flag. Not being loved by all is one thing; being hated by all is another. Ask yourself, is she eager to spread gossip at work? Is she telling you someone else's personal information? If she is ready and willing to give up the goods so soon, what will she do with your secrets?

After you determine she is safe enough to hang out with in public, try a neutral event that includes other coworkers. A ball game, a restaurant, dancing, or a trivia night.

Why include other women?

Primarily, because there is safety in numbers. If for any reason things go from "hell yes" to "oh hell no," you have other people to mediate and handle the problem. The last thing you want is to be stuck by yourself with a woman you barely know, in a bar you've never been to, watching her get sloppy drunk and wondering how you are going to get her home.

Secondly, if you already have a core group of friends you hang with at work, it is good to know if she can be included in group events or if she has to be seen individually.

Lastly, this method will confirm whether your outside personalities are compatible. Do you party the same? Do you enjoy similar things? Are the activities she is into interesting to you? If she is a super fit chick who spends the bulk of her time doing physical activities, and your idea of a great time is anything involving music, there may be limited opportunities for you to fit one another into your schedules. Unless you are willing to participate in each other's interests, you may end up being just work friends.

If during your relationship you feel comfortable inviting her to your wedding or attending her baby shower, know that you are potentially exposing yourself to not just her, but to the entire staff of your workplace. When things go bad with a work friend, most often the experiences you had outside of work somehow make their rounds into office gossip. Suddenly everyone knows what happened in Vegas, even though, for so many reasons, it should have stayed there. Not every woman will jump at the chance to embarrass you. She may only tell her other office friend a story that she finds the tea too salacious to keep to herself. Word of mouth could spread faster than you can walk to the water cooler to hear yourself being talked about.

I do not like to categorize work friends as mixing business with pleasure, because if your friendship does not work out after combining the two worlds, you cannot un-mix things. Especially if you did not end on good terms. It is likely that one of you will carry some resentment back into your job and make things uncomfortable. However, if you walk into the relationship treating it as something separate from your work relationship, you can maintain your business integrity before, during, and after.

No woman is worth risking or ruining your career for. Every friend you make at work and then integrate into your life is a separate risk. Riskier than a standard friend, because she is so close to your pocketbook. Protect your money, protect your position, and most importantly, protect your heart.

I know you can feel powerless over your work climate. You just want to go to work, do your job, and leave. All the politics that happen in between clouds your purpose and drains your energy. If you have a toxic workplace, you may not be able to just quit or instantly find a new job. During the time you are stuck in that environment, remove much of the dysfunction by utilizing the Three Rules and by being mindful of whom you associate with. Do not let a person or job have control over your entire life. Despite what the world tell you, you were not born just to survive through occupation. You are defined by more than your career and worth more than the dollars on your paycheck. Live as though you have options, because dammit, you do.

PART FOUR:

THE DETOX

As we detoxify our relationships, we want to be armed with the tools to replenish ourselves with quality associations that are mutually beneficial and rewarding. I believe in the power of love between friends immensely. The presence and support of my friends throughout the years has made me a better woman in every way possible. I do not want women to read this book and walk away feeling like they'll never be satisfied within a friendship. I do not want anyone to finish convinced that women or friendships are more hassle than they are worth. Because when a friendship is good, you have an awesome force behind you.

This is the light at the end of the tunnel. I could have talked about the good stuff at the beginning, but I like to end on a high note. What are the most important aspects of friendship? I mean the life-applicable definition of friendship, not just what you can find in *Merriam-Webster*, where the definition of friendship only requires friendly feelings or a sense of liking. If that were the case, I am best friends with Starbucks. Both the baristas and the actual store. This broad, but limited, definition doesn't indicate that friendship should be happy or healthy overall. The motivation behind defining toxic and recognizing toxicity is not only to remove it, but also to replace it with better relationships.

Defining what you allow and require is just a matter of being prepared. How to be a good friend seems like common sense. You assume that it should be second nature, or so obvious that it does not need clarification, but it does. Not to set a stagnant, one-size-fits-all standard, but to be a continuous marker and reminder that shapes your life. You are now demanding more from yourself, your friends, and the world around you. But, what does that look like in practice?

Where to start? At the beginning of course. It is a lot easier to keep your friendship from becoming toxic than it is to bring it back from its unhealthy state. There are key elements of friendship to understand and consider before you even begin. You must know who you are and what you expect. Determining friendship compatibility is a must. Opposites may attract, but they aren't always healthy. You have to be prepared to navigate through calm and rough waters without abandoning the (friend)ship. Your social life depends on you being able to talk through and forgive the inevitable issues that will occur.

What if I am already healthy?

What do I do once I shed my toxic ways?

After you have stopped the behaviors that prevented you from being your best self, you replace them with improved and more beneficial practices. You take everything you have learned about loving yourself and the women around you and continue to build upon that through action.

START HEALTHY

Limitless Love

With friendship comes pressure to perform:

You don't want to disappoint them.

You don't want them to stop caring about you.

You are invested in their happiness.

You enjoy having them in your life.

Therefore, you go out of the way to make your friends happy. You help them achieve their goals and inform them that their dreams are possible. You compliment them and console them. You do this all to the wear the badge of honor called friendship. This is the kind of energy you should expect to give to yourself. Being your own best friend means treating yourself with the same passion and persistence as you treat your treasured friends.

Recall the Toxic R.U.L.E. *L* is for Loving. As discussed, loving is pivotal when it comes to the process of shedding the worst of your former self. However, loving becomes even more pertinent in maintaining your best self. Beyond appearance, accomplishments, and accolades, you have to really love the person you are, for what you are.

Without embellishments, extra adornment, or honestly with pretense, you have to wake up every morning and not only appreciate the woman you are; you have to actively nurture her. You have to be your number one cheerleader, your main support system, the first person to build you up, and the last person to consult on major decisions. You cannot say you are your own best friend without treating yourself like your best friend. The knowledge that you, the world you live in, and the people you interact with can all be toxic is pointless, if you do not use that information to benefit yourself.

You are square one, you are home base, you are the most important person in your emotional and mental health.

Be *good* to you.

Be kind to you.

Love you.

If you determine why you are likely to run yourself ragged for someone else, you will begin to clarify why you must now treat your personal relationship the same way.

Do you want to make yourself proud?

Do you want to take care of yourself?

Are you invested in your own happiness?

Are you enjoying your life?

Make sure all these answers are "yes" before you begin to pour your efforts into anyone else. Loving the woman you are keeps you from needing to find your definition of self anywhere else. Being your own best friend means establishing a tether between your thoughts and core that cannot be unraveled by life's ups and downs. This level of undaunted self-love is crucial to succeeding on your journey.

Maintain the Me

Practice continuous self-care. A combination of self-love and self-care makes a non-toxic existence possible. Life can suck. It can be awesome, but sometimes, it can really suck. I'm talking Starbucks messed up your order, the AUX cord broke on your way to work, your boss is being an extra ass-hatty, you forgot to bring something for the potluck, you were stuck between two accidents on the way home, your package from Amazon was stolen, and you didn't defrost the chicken for dinner... sucky. On those days, we start to question ourselves, our value, our purpose, and everything else about our existence. Sometimes the best thing you can do for others is take care of yourself to ensure the best you is being presented to the world.

If I am sleep deprived, on an emotional eating binge, or having a lapse in my confidence, I am not a wonderful person. As I become more critical of myself, I become more critical of others. In knowingly good women, I do not search for the light in the darkness of their words and actions. I get overwhelmed with being overwhelmed, and miss out on dates, cancel on appointments, and stop practicing good communication. Once I lose sight of my own worth, I devalue my surroundings and the people in them. Initially I was under the impression that these emotional ailments were the problem, when the actual issue was not giving myself the time I needed to be good at being myself.

Leisure does not always look the same. Unfortunately, it can't always be a girl's trip to Bora Bora. You need to identify as many small-scale energy boosters within your life as possible for internal maintenance. Establish an arsenal that can be at your disposal whenever you need it. Having a variety guarantees that you are never without an option. Personally, I am partial to a glass of wine, a few moments of dark and silence, listening to music, going to see my family, and even stretching. Each one can be just the thing to strengthen my soul. Find your fixes. Keep them within arm's reach. Use them constantly. The better you are to yourself, the greater the chances you will have the energy, will, and passion to be better to others.

Deal Breakers

There are women you will meet and think are amazing. They are amazing. However, every amazing woman does not need to be your friend. You may have to admire them from afar. Why ever pass up on an amazing woman? Two words: Deal Breakers. You don't have to be identical, but building a connection without considering your compatibility is irresponsible. If you move too differently, it is okay to not attempt to overcome that hurdle.

Understanding your friend's morals and ideals is essential at the beginning of a friendship. I'm not saying you should confer with a list of what you will and won't do, complete with a recording secretary to email minutes at adjournment. However, since even with access to a dictionary we all manage to have different definitions of acceptable friendship behavior, you may want to know what kind of person you're getting into relationship with. We can't assume that whomever we become friends with is living by the same code of ethics we are. If there are actions that our friends endorse that we are vehemently against, it isn't always healthy for our own sanity to turn the other cheek.

Make no apologies for limiting of the behaviors you allow in your life; just be consistent. If you cannot associate with people who drink in excess, it might be difficult for you to be close with someone who is imbibes regularly. This might appear an evident conclusion, but women will make capacitance for friends even when it goes against what they stand for. Be sure you understand not only who you are friends with, but also what your friends do. You cannot be disappointed when she acts as she sees fit and it contradicts what you are okay with, specifically if she has always been that way and you have accepted that behavior before.

Try not to write off someone from the first issue; see if there is a pattern of behavior that you are uncomfortable with instead of an instance. You shouldn't be rushing to dismiss quickly. The goal is to establish a relationship with someone who is like-minded, or compatible, not critique, criticize, and condemn every minor infraction. Deal Breakers are finding your bottom line and not participating in relationships below it, not being judgmental and closed off from women who are different from you.

Go with the Flow

Friendships are not static; they are flexible, they grow, and they need pruning. That means you must be willing to share more than you receive and not count favors along the way. It requires too much work to keep score on who has done what and where, when you should just be happy with the why, because you guys are friends. When things start to go haphazard, we want to be able to rest on our foundations. Friends can play a large role in that stability by being allies for your goals, ambitions, and daily life.

That means turning on their light so we can shine, expanding to protect you as your emotional bodyguard, knowing when they should yell at you, and when they should whisper instead. The only way that seamless transition can occur is for there to be an understood willingness for you to do the same. Friendship can't function with the condition that they do it first or only as much as you have already done. When there are highs, ride them, and when there are lows, survive them. Learn to prioritize your friendship more than individual actions. That focus on the unit is what makes it work.

Let fluidity guide how you put things into perspective. Don't constantly complain about your horrible day at work, when you know your friend is struggling to find a job. You have to know to give pause to sharing all your wedding details when her boyfriend literally just packed up and moved out last night. Going with the flow is what motivates you to not bring up the lavish shopping spree you just went on, when they just mentioned that their bank account is in the negative.

Flow requires an intentional awareness and careful consideration, focused on the appreciation that friendship is never defined by what you give or what you get. (Hello Martyr and Opportunist.) You are investing in a person, a feeling, and a combined existence. Experience it without the tit for tat. Or else it'll cheapen the quality of the friendship you're creating.

Building Boxes

Understand the multiple layers, circles, or tiers of friendships you can have. Many have only one idea of friendship, which can be limiting when building a comprehensive tribe of women around you. It is okay to have different relationships with various women. It is okay to share selectively and have distinct associations. We are multidimensional creatures. To expect one friend to satisfy all the complexity within us requires a tall order to fill. Find freedom in yourself by giving leeway to your friends. One person does not have to be your everything. Separate that responsibility amongst however many people you need to feel complete. There are levels to friendship. Take full advantage of them, and box them into different categories.

Limitation seems like a negative. However, in this instance, limitation is a mixture of realism and protection. I want you to have the best relationships possible. Sometimes we can be overzealous in the weight we place on one person. Practice boxing people so you have realistic expectations of what those people can satisfy within your life. Boxes don't have to be constricting, they can be very comfortable when used correctly. If, or when, they become uncomfortable, you can modify accordingly.

You are more likely to stay happy within the relationship when the results match your expectations. For example, if you have a friend who is very reserved in her emotions and actions, it would be unreasonable to think she would be ideal for the new improv class you want to try.

Sure, it's not that she can never be anything other than reserved, but to expect her to go against her nature because it would be fun for you is unrealistic. You probably know another, more outgoing friend who would share that enjoyment more equally. An associate, regardless of how close you are, who has expressed interest in performing arts would be better suited to go with you. Your best friends do not have to share everything with you.

Boxing people also allows for diversifying your friendship portfolio. Learn to take advantage of the best of your friends without penalizing them for the things that do not match you exactly. There is a reason behind the advice to never put all your eggs in one basket. One heavy basket to lug around only leads to a stronger probability of fumbling that basket and cracking shells. Protect your eggs; box your friends.

Communication and Connection

Communication can make a bad thing better or a good thing worse, depending on how well you do it. You absolutely must be able to talk to your friends. How else can you thank them, compliment them, exchange ideas, or work out problems? Everyone wants wonderful communication, yet, the moment you tell someone you want to work on achieving that, they start to shut down. Suddenly, it feels like some arduous and lengthy task that will require too much effort. Guess what, communication is just talking. When you need to work on your communication, it means you need express, listen, and explain more. You need to improve your speech. Being vocally present in your friendship can only strengthen it.

I completely understand how technology has and will continue to change how we communicate with one another. I know people who refuse to talk on the phone unless it is an emergency. I have seen people have entire conversations about personal plans in a comment thread rather than just discussing it offline. I am not here to tell you how to talk. Do what works for you, but remain willing to diversify your methods of communication. Should you find that the methods you currently use don't allow you to have the depth of conversations needed to retain the quality of your friendships, switch it up.

You might have a friend who struggles to text you back because she is either busy at work or busy at home with her family. When you don't know how she manages to brush her teeth in morning between corralling all her kids and shuttling them off to different schools, you may need to call her to catch up. It might be more efficient to have a thirty-minute conversation every two weeks than to exchange halfhearted texts over the month that amount in nothing more than "Hey, how are you doing" over and over again, regardless of whether that is your preferred method of communication.

If you are anything like me, you are also busy. Not "I watch *Grey's* and *Scandal* on Thursday, *Game of Thrones* and *The Walking Dead* on Sunday" busy. I mean your weekends can be booked two months in advance busy. I get it. Scheduling life is difficult. However you have time in your day that you don't utilize to catch up with friends—time that may otherwise be wasted.

Suggestions: Do you have a long commute? Make that your time to catch up with friends whom you know are also in transit. It is a great way to distract yourself from the temptation of road rage, hands-free of course, and enjoy some high-quality chatting. Before you know it, you are both home and happy to still be connected. All you missed out on was the same songs you listen to every day. Give Beyoncé a break for a good cause.

Unless you have switched completely to delivery and meal prep services, you still shop for necessities like food and toilet paper. Why not meet a friend monthly or bi-monthly to stock up on household staples? If you think going to Costco or Trader Joe's is a good time alone, it will be like a party when you have your favorite girl by your side. Including your friends in your life is about more than scheduling outings than can easily be dismissed as unnecessary. It is about meeting at Target to pick up trash bags and tampons and spending a little too much time in the dollar section because you're lost in conversation.

Keep a loose mental schedule of checking in with your friends. Depending on how often you typically talk, make a social calendar to ensure you have kept up with them. Have specific days of the week, or times of the day, when you make sure to communicate in some form. Like, *Talk to Tasha on Tuesdays.* If you haven't talked to her since the last Tuesday, check in. Every two weeks, it can be "Melissa Monday," and so on, even for the friends who don't offer alliteration. It's a soft reminder to reach out if you've been slacking with keeping in touch.

Please stop sharing those ridiculous memes that brag, "Real friends can not talk for years and just pick up at the same spot." The sentiment is fact wrapped in fiction. Yes, you can have a friend whom you temporarily lose touch with and, once you regain contact, continue the relationship as though that break never existed. When we are going through transitions and are being pulled in different directions, a large chunk of time can pass before we realize we haven't talked to our friend for longer than we'd imagined. In these cases, when you finally get the chance to have that long conversation or much needed brunch, you are not starting your relationship all over. However, if your relationship is based on long periods of time in which you do not communicate at all, followed by a short, inconsistent burst of talking, you are no longer friends. You are two women with a past and no present.

That does not mean you are enemies. You certainly can continue to check in on one another periodically, speak to one another occasionally, and want the best for one another. But friendship requires investment. It requires actual input. You have to nurture it, grow it, prioritize it. Stop diluting the concept of friendship with half-ass associations. Just categorize it for what it is, not what you want it to be. But most importantly, stop trying to convince the world that you manage to achieve the impossible: a great friendship with a person you never talk to.

Above All Else, Forgive

Forgive Yourself First

Even the best of us mess up. You know, the whole being human thing means you literally can never be perfect. Messed up on your wing eyeline? Meh, can't get it every time. Have some rolls when you sit down, even though you have a six-pack? Human. Can solve every math equation without any effort but cannot ever remember whether to use affect or effect? Totally normal. So as a perfection-resistant woman, it is inevitable that your toxic behavior will spill out uncontrollably and destroy your amazing record.

Not if, but when, this happens, your first reaction may be to rush to apologize to whomever you hurt. We have been trained to believe an apology is the undefeated champion of fixing things. I agree, but only if the apology you give is to yourself first. You need internal reconciliation through acceptance of what happened and the role you played, before any apology can be beneficial to someone else.

Forgiveness is personal. When you forgive someone or ask to be forgiven, it is for your benefit. You cannot depend on the reaction of your apology to the person you've slighted to absolve you of your guilt. Guilt is also personal. This does not mean that you make no efforts to apologize to the other person, or people, in the situation. This does not mean that if you apologize and they do not accept it that you do not try to find another way to rectify your actions. It means that is secondary to the work you do inside first.

Contrary to popular belief, you do not owe yourself guilt; you owe yourself growth. I repeat, growth over guilt. When you can identify what went wrong in your toxic tirade, your responsibility is not to then rerun the infraction over and over in your mind. That does nothing but waste your time and energy. What you should be doing is identifying how you can grow from it. Run through the toxic R.U.L.E. and remember it is about evolving beyond that moment.

I stress doing this before you seek forgiveness from the other party because that forgiveness may never come. After you have apologized, offered multiple ways to fix things, or begged and pleaded, should you need to go that far… guess what? She may still not forgive you. Then what? Do you stay in an eternal state of penitence? Do you stay married to that remorse 'til death do you part? No. Most mistakes aren't a life sentence. You will have to come to terms with your indiscretion on your own. You will have to absorb the weight of your actions and live with yourself. All without ever getting the all-clear from her.

Despite all your growth, you may run into a time when you are not as healthy as you should be. Sometimes our ability to manage ourselves can ebb and flow. In those phases, you may burn bridges, alienate yourself, and offend people. Regret and remorse might not be the R&R you were looking for, but it can be what you end up with. Grow from that point, for yourself. I am not advocating careless or reckless behavior because you know your forgiveness is the only one that matters. I am advocating that when you put in the work to be the best you, the times that you do falter, forgiving yourself is the only thing that matters.

Working Through Forgiveness

Forgiveness is a process that starts with the desire to move on. It is not forgetting what has occurred. It is not saying that the person has made up for what they did. It is you, saying to yourself, *I am ready to move beyond the feeling of this offense.* Forgiveness is too often depicted as the culmination of an apology instead of journey it is. Just because you decide to forgive does not mean your emotions will let you get to that point immediately. It may require time, but it does not require assistance.

Forgiving and moving forward can occur together or separately. If you decided to remain friends with someone after they have hurt you, reminding them how they have hurt you whenever it is convenient is not a healthy way to approach forgiveness. Yes, there is often atonement that must occur to fix a relationship, but they cannot give you a reason to forgive them. They can request and work to get you to continue to invest in the friendship, but I cannot stress enough: Forgiveness is a decision you have to make for yourself.

Forgiveness is for your benefit and your freedom. The problem is, although I know you read that, and I presented a pretty compelling reason why it would be a good idea, some of you will insist that harboring all the negativity that someone has transferred to you is somehow benefiting you. It isn't. For those of you who remain hardheaded and hard-hearted, I make this one request: If you are holding onto something that is over seven years old. LET IT GO.

Just like the moment that initial college credit card you racked up, knowing you couldn't pay it, would fall off your credit report. Let it go. You know that it is no longer an accurate reflection of your financial responsibility or capability. Yet you are still treating anything that anyone has done to you like it is fresh and relevant. Unless that person has continued to lower their friendship credit score by continuing to be irresponsible within the friendship, the ship has sailed on acting like it is impacting your relationship now. Seven years, that is all you get. After that you either need to move on within the relationship or move on from the friendship completely.

STAY HEALTHY

Share the Wealth

Give compliments without reserve. They are not akin to the good china brought out for special occasions. If you see someone wearing a great shirt or amazing shoes, why are you not telling her? I get compliments infrequently. I don't know why; I am clearly exuding awesome on such a regular basis that I should be swimming in them. Still, that never stops me from recognizing and acknowledging another woman's glow.

If we just told one another the truth, "You are beautiful," "You are kind," or "Your art is so dope," then we could stop this farce that we universally hate on each other all the time.

Get comfortable with lifting other women up just because you can. You never need an invitation to be a personal cheerleader to a stranger. There are so many social benefits to giving verbal high fives.

First, believe it or not, you will feel good about yourself. I always walk away a little happier when I see the smile on another woman's face after giving her a compliment.

Second, they usually walk away with a brighter beam in their eyes. You may have just taken her toxic level down a notch, or she may in turn compliment someone else. Energy is fluid. Positivity is transferable. Give some of your joy to someone else, and watch it multiply.

Lastly, someone else may overhear your kind words. Before you know it, you may have unconsciously started a tsunami of good vibes that will impact women you don't even know. This kind of positivity grows our community. There is no such thing as too much empowerment between women. Start your personal efforts today.

Observation Versus Absorption

We have all been there. A girlfriend asks for your advice on an important matter, and you pull out your premium thoughts. I mean the really good ones, representing the concern and love you have for her. You spin sentences so beautiful, they are like an acrylic painting of the essence of your soul. She thanks you sincerely for your support, your input, and your constant presence as pillar of positivity in her life. Then she ignores everything you told her and proceeds to set a dumpster fire instead.

Moments like this, you try to remind yourself that you are dealing with a flawed person. A woman with her own thoughts and desires about how she wants this situation to play out. She asked for your opinion, and it was never a legal decree of what she had to do. You gave a valid effort to steer her in the right direction, but ultimately it is her life, and she can make her own choices.

It's annoying, but, typically, not a reason to cut her off. Even when two months, two weeks, and two days later she is in the same place, asking you the same questions, and you can't figure out how to say the same thing any differently. So you try to re-spin the wheel you already twirled. You cut a few adjectives, add a few different examples, and remind her how much she is valued and loved. You're certain that this time you got through to her. But you didn't. After another hour-long conversation, it takes a matter of moments before she has forgotten every syllable you have said and proceeded to set, yep, another blaze to her life. At this point, her world is burning to the ground around her. You are trying your best to extend her a facemask, some water, a fire extinguisher, anything, and she is just complacent dancing around in the chaos, like the smoke isn't choking her.

Beyond her questionable state of mind, for you, it is becoming taxing to try to help her. Being this close to the fire isn't safe anymore, and you are starting to notice the charring from being so close to her problem.

What should you do? Exactly what you learned in elementary school during those fire drills. Stop, drop, and roll away. You should not sacrifice yourself beyond reason to stay in a hazardous situation that she is content with. You have to understand that it is unhealthy to be too invested in a situation you have no control over. Begin separating the acts of observing and absorbing what is going on. In the instances when friends ask for support for show and not for actual help, you have to stop offering up the best of yourself.

Does this mean you stop being there, or you stop listening? Not necessarily. It means you stop caring about that situation more than she cares to change it. And when she asks for advice again, you tell her honestly, you have none outside of what you have already given. You remind her that she is loved, but most importantly that she should decide for herself what she needs to do if she is unhappy. Do not make any additional comments or give any additional opinions until she makes some changes on her own.

Her opinion and actions are the only ones that matter. Not the great references, data, and optics you provide, proving your opinion is valid and most helpful. Not your emotional pleas of sound judgment and undeniable truth. None of that matters until she decides it does. You have absorbed enough of the residual smoke. It is time you observe what occurs from a safe distance, with your fingers crossed and your fire truck ready, in the event she honestly needs you more than she needs to waste your time.

Is that what she wants? Absolutely not. But she needs to be aware that she is spreading her toxicity and respect your emotional boundaries. People are often so wrapped up in their own issues, they unintentionally affect those around them while they are in turmoil. Sometimes, they just to need to be brought back to your mutual reality. One that does not revolve around themselves or that problem.

Now a good, non-toxic friend would take this as a learning experience and adjust herself accordingly. However, not everyone will have a positive, or even neutral, reaction to your setting boundaries. Remind yourself, just as you have reminded your friend countless times during her entire ordeal, that you are loved, supported, and have control over your situation. Everything isn't worth a consistent investment; understand that's okay.

Trigger Warnings

Stop setting yourself up for failure. For real. Stop. If you know someone has the ability to take you to an emotional space you don't want to enter, don't accept that invite. Decline the opportunity to RSVP to the toxic party. That can mean direct avoidance or little to no interaction with someone. Not because you cannot control yourself, but to ensure you always have control over yourself.

Growth will reveal all these new techniques, motivations, and methods to stay healthy. The way you carry yourself will change. The foundation your mood is built on will be reinforced with every step you take to detox. The problem with all these new emotional muscles you've built is that you are bound to want to flex them. You're going to want to show off your new and improved resolve. It's tempting to prove to yourself and everyone else that you know how amazingly non-toxic you are. You want to keep patting yourself on the back for progress, but don't exhaust yourself unnecessarily in precarious situations just to satisfy your ego. It isn't worth the risk, because you are bound to slip up at some point.

When you are fortunate enough to refrain from a problem once, walk away and stay away. Don't assume it will be that easy to control yourself the next time. Russian roulette is a dangerous game for a reason. If the possibility of losing control isn't compelling enough for you, or if you are so convinced you can handle anything and everyone without losing your cool, ask yourself, why waste the effort? Why not avoid fatiguing those awesome new muscles for situations that aren't worth it. If you need an adrenaline rush, go skydiving, do CrossFit, test your fortitude trying West African dance, try replicating a makeup tutorial video, attempt to buy Adele concert tickets before they sell out, or perform at an amateur comedy show. Do anything but risk your mental health by not paying attention to your own trigger warnings.

This can be a sacrifice. There are people I have not spoken to in a decade. I avoid any interaction with them. Sometimes I miss events to miss seeing them; I know better. On the surface I could maintain a pleasant tone or forced smile, but it would take one potentially misused word, a slight inflection on the wrong syllable, to unleash my true negative feelings. I've learned it is better that I don't even give myself room to fail.

Respect Yourself by Respecting Others

Let's be real. Sometimes it feels good to hurt other people. If we are going to be completely honest with ourselves, there are some ugly facts we have to rationalize. When you feel slighted, hurt, harmed, or disrespected by someone, it feels almost necessary to even the score. No matter how much you are told two wrongs don't make a right, the temptation of retaliation is too strong. I am willing to bet after your last confrontation, the two things that crossed your mind first were what you wished you had said and how good it felt to say the things you did. The third may very well be remorse for some other things that occurred during the fight, but while you are still riding that high, what you are focused on is the quality of your attack, and asking yourself, *Did I win?*

Arguments will happen. Some arguments need to happen. But there is a way to argue, even heatedly, without crossing a line of respectfulness that should always be recognized. Without debate, keep your hands to yourself. If you are not protecting yourself or someone else in self-defense, there is no reason to disrespect someone's body by fighting them. That is the greatest display of your inability to control yourself. Your opinions deserve a better chance of being expressed than you overshadowing them with assault. Therefore, when I am discussing respect, assume that a physical attack has not and will not occur. Really ladies, you don't need a mug shot.

Do not call someone out of their name. I understand, it feels like there are some people who *need* to hear what you think they are. It can even feel like they don't merit be called the name their momma gave them. I promise you, I know the delight in dousing someone in a flickering of fact-based vulgarities. Calling some "deserving" person obscenities can give you a ridiculous, shameful sense of satisfaction. Like the whole-mouth feel you get from a delicious piece of food after you weren't able to chew because you had your wisdom teeth taken out. I call it the umami of arguing. Seriously, it can be that good. In the end, it is just a poor representation of your ability to defend your argument. Your position will get lost in the cornucopia of curse words, no matter how creatively you integrate them.

When they look back at the exchange, all your sound judgment and reasoning will not be visible through the smoke still burning from the flames of your heated words. Don't fight yourself while you're fighting them. Respecting them, even when it is inconvenient, is a testament to the respect you have for yourself. Every fight doesn't have to be foul, and every foul doesn't have to be flagrant.

There is always a non-confrontational way of addressing issues with someone. If you feel they are having a difficult time grasping why you are upset, try to isolate specific behaviors and how they make you feel. Sometimes people fail to see the big picture because they are busy nitpicking at the details. It is counterproductive because you never solve the real problem. Break it down to the action and the result; then build from there. It isn't easy having someone marginalize your perspective or discount your point of view. However, if your goal is to be understood and to come to some form of truce, you may have to try an approach that doesn't feel as satisfying, because it will be more effective.

Embracing "Extreme" Measures

These measures should not be considered extreme in the first place. There is nothing wrong or unusual about seeking external advice from a professional or counselor can provide an unbiased opinion, advice, insight, or support. Yes, our friends provide a helpful hand, an empty shoulder, and an open ear. Sometimes all those body parts are not enough, and we need more help than anyone around us can give. Sometimes we get stuck and cannot help ourselves. Sometimes we just want to talk to another person who is not connected to our lives. Sometimes it is more convenient. Sometimes it is absolutely necessary. Sometimes we are left with no other choice. And sometimes it can be the thing to save us. Do not stop yourself from seeking professional help.

There is a reason psychiatrists, therapists, and counselors exist. We need them. Take advantage of whatever sources of support you have available to you, whenever you need it, to be as healthy as possible.

There are many discussions taking place on how to eliminate the stigma of mental illness. Part of the discussion includes taking away the negative depiction of mental health professionals. That is a very important step to breaking down the wall between us and better lives. However, mental illness is not the only reason we can need professional help. We need to stop privately admitting our struggles, and publicly acknowledge we are deciding to take care of ourselves with assistance.

You may need one session. You may need ten. You may need continuous care that includes psychology and psychiatry long term. Never hesitate to get more help, and more importantly, never question a friend who finds comfort in professional hands. Nothing is too extreme when it comes to helping yourself.

No type of person is off limits for turning to. You may just need to speak to a guidance counselor or religious leader. Community groups, hotlines, and spiritual units are tools like any other to use to your advantage. Whatever it is, whomever it is, embrace the process of healing yourself. Own it, and don't allow anyone else to question the methods you are willing to take to be okay. External toxicity cannot be managed if internal toxicity is not acknowledged. Don't be afraid to walk down the road to improving your life just because the path is new, different, or includes someone holding your hand.

Closing the Door

Another over-memed quote is: "You have three types of friends in life: Friends for a reason, friends for a season, and friends for a lifetime." Unlike the communication meme, this one is completely true. Some people are friends for now, and others forever. It doesn't make them less relevant or important, it just means they were not lasting. The one thing this meme doesn't address is the exit. Since I can understand how restrictive meme space can be, let us unpack that concept.

We know that the ending of a friendship is not something we imagined when it began. Unless you are super famous, or super kinky, chances are, you don't have a lawyer on staff drafting non-disclosure agreements that state exactly what will happen at the culmination of your friendship. Even if you had the forethought to pre-nup your friendship, which would be weird, it typically addresses possessions and public statements, not private feelings. Meaning, even the best-planned, well-executed departure from the friend zone will leave a ton of feelings to muddle through.

Probability dictates you aren't unfriending because you think the best of her. It can be the case, but it serves as the rare exception. Typically, one or both of you decided there was a fatal flaw in your friendship and it was time to cut your losses and move on. Throughout this book I have encouraged reflection before and during that moment, but what about after? Instinct will have you look at what she did wrong first. That is a fine place to start. Do not let it end there. Move into the space where you then analyze yourself and what you did to contribute to the demise of your friendship.

Then, end on a good note. Unless your friendship stopped at the exact moment it started, or the woman you were friends with was a psychopath, you had to have some shared positive memories. Don't throw those away with the friendship. That is your happiness to keep, even when things between you go sour. It is important that we learn how to retain the good occasions, feelings, and memories.

These parts of your failed relationship matter because they remind you that you were not crazy for caring in the first place. It reinforces that your investment was not a waste of time. Not everything that does not work out is a bad investment. That friendship failure has a valuable lesson littered amongst the shambles. She still made you laugh, she still listened to you when you cried, and if she hurt you along the way, she still helped make you the person you are now. A little stronger, hopefully a little wiser, but definitely better off through the experience.

When you leave the negativity in the relationship and do not let it carry over, you experience the power that a positive perception can have. Yes, you can support them without being a part of the decisions they make or the life they lead. You can applaud their accomplishments from afar, send condolences when appropriate, and still no longer consider them your friend. You celebrate celebrities and strangers you do not know all the time; don't act like you can't still be happy for her. Okay, you guys were not compatible as friends. Unless she committed a horrendous act against you, let it, and the bad vibes from it, go. Separate does not mean enemies, and your ending does not mean you have to begin despising them. There will be times when that is all you want to do, but there is no gratification in grudging.

It will take longer for some friendships to move beyond the acts that tore you apart to remembering the connection that brought you together. Still try. Eventually, you will understand the freedom and peace that comes with leaving the past in the past. Show appreciation for the gift of goodbye by returning forgiveness back into the universe.

MY TOXIC STORY PT. 2

I have, well I had, a college friend whom I haven't spoken to since her wedding, for which I was a bridesmaid. I will give you a minute to absorb that while I give the back-story.

When I got married, I rushed into the idea of it feeling normal. I didn't have wonderment of the honeymoon phase, because I wanted to prove to myself that I was so ready to be married that nothing would in my relationship. I regret it. Whenever someone gets married now, I wait for them to talk to me first. Not because I don't want to know everything about them since the "I do," but because I don't want to be an extra person rushing them back to their new "normal" life.

When we did not talk initially, I wasn't bothered or worried. I assumed she was resting, relaxing, and wanting to be in love land. When I didn't get a wedding recap or a thank you card for my wedding gift. I didn't mind. Things happen.

During this time, I was also toiling through my first pregnancy. She was aware of this, and leading up to her wedding, she expressed that she was overwhelmed with other women and their pregnancies. Although I felt her response to be dismissive, I tucked away those hurt feelings. Weddings can be stressful. I assured her my pregnancy wouldn't be an issue and it wouldn't interfere with me being a bridesmaid. I was partially wrong. My pregnancy was physically demanding from the beginning, with complications starting as soon as I found out. Even though I could have used her support, I understood she was not emotionally available to give any, and I did not discuss my struggles.

On her wedding day I showed up on time, smiled on queue, and tried my best to hide what felt like a slow death. By the time 10:00 rolled around that night, I had thrown up multiple times, broken my shoe, and had the opportunity to see her dance the night away with the love of her life. It was a beautiful wedding. She was a stunning bride. And I was praying to get home before I passed out. When I decided to leave at the same time as some mutual friends, she was wrapped in the loving arms of her husband. So, I did not interrupt her to say goodbye.

I know what some of you are thinking, how could you not say goodbye?! Easy, she is not someone who lets you leave a party until after last call. Considering her mostly annoyed response to me telling her I was pregnant to begin with, I did not, and still do not, see telling her I had to go for that reason going over well. At all. I decided, I would just catch up with her later.

Later never happened. When I contacted her a few months down the line with an urgent medical question because she is a physician, I prefaced it with a sincere apology for bothering her when I knew she was still in her love zone, but I was desperate.

Desperate like laying in the hallway unable to get off the floor because I could not walk.

Desperate like calling the ER begging to be admitted. When she replied to my text, she was very professional and short. I didn't initially notice this because I was distracted by my discomfort. Considering the communication seal was broken anyway, I attempted to reach out to her via text a few days afterward just to see how she was doing. I thought we could catch up, or even better, meet up. Difference was, this time I caught on to her text tone. I recognized that she was not reciprocating, her responses were dry, and she was not engaging in conversation. I was taken aback and confused as hell. I didn't want to overreact, so I assumed she had a lot going on. I let it go.

When she declined to come to my baby shower, opting instead to send a card-less gift card, I knew it was more than just life getting in the way. Anyone who knows me knows I would rather have the card than the gift card. This was intentional. This was a deliberate statement. She wasn't messing with me.

This wasn't the first instance of conflict in our friendship. We had a nasty falling out shortly after undergrad. Therefore, before going forward, I had to look back at what happened then to ensure I wouldn't repeat the same mistakes. The first time we had a falling, out I immediately erased her from my life. Deleted her number and unfriended her on social media. I wanted nothing to do with her. It was a rash and hasty decision, made at the height of my anger. I didn't give her any leeway, and it was a poor decision. We both moved on, grew, and continued to thrive separately.

After about three years, through some twist of fate, we reconnected. Without going into the event that had initially led to the end of our friendship, we jumped right back into it like we had pressed pause instead of stop. I held onto a small piece of regret over how quickly I dismissed her before, and made it a point to be more understanding should another conflict ever arise.

I was at the height of my self-reflection stage and overzealously committed to being better to her this go around. If she called me, busy or not, I answered. I constantly followed up with her and supported her as she went through various educational and social changes. Friendship is never a straight line. I had no problem giving her a little more than she gave me, because she needed it and I had it to give. She was a bridesmaid in my wedding, I sent her care packages while she was away, I flew across the country for her graduation, and upon her return to California, I was first in line to help her with anything for her wedding. In many ways I was a better friend to her than she was to me. But I also failed her. In my attempt to be considerate and understanding, I also enabled her often-selfish behavior.

So why have I not spoken to her since 2015? Why has she never met my children or asked how I am doing since her wedding day? I couldn't tell you. I can guess a lot. But, only she knows the reasoning behind deciding to no longer be my friend and never telling me why. I have replayed our last face-to-face interactions over in my mind, more than a few times, and have yet to find a flaw so damning to warrant a complete erasure of my presence. Could she have been upset that I left without talking to her? Possibly. I'm sure she told me "bye" at my wedding, so that could have hurt her feelings. However, even if she hadn't, it wouldn't have mattered enough for me to stop being her friend.

More importantly, by the time I realized she had decided she was no longer my friend, and not just enjoying the beauty of newlywed bliss, I didn't need to know the reason why. She didn't care enough to express any issue she had with me. She didn't care to continue our friendship by giving me the opportunity to explain myself for whatever I had done. She didn't care enough to work things out. She didn't care about any of the positivity and love I showered her in beforehand. She didn't care to try.

She just didn't care, and that's all I really needed to know.

I was not going to chase after a grown woman to find out why she was giving me the silent treatment. I could not solely burden the upkeep of our friendship. Therefore, I let her finish what she started on her own.

Over time red flags I had ignored and information I had missed came to light. Decisions made before and after rekindling our friendship were put into a new perspective when aligned with her most recent actions. All these things helped me transition into our new, friendless existence. I got into a new flow of things and realized that I was just fine. Her presence, or lack thereof, didn't matter. I don't mean that in a cruel way. That isn't an insult to her. Just, when it came down to it, whatever we had was not as pivotal or pertinent as I thought it to be.

Although I was not the person to initiate the conclusion of our friendship, I had complete control of how I responded. Instead of tearing her down, I slowly phased her out. Instead of focusing so much on the ending of things, and remaining frustrated with feeling mistreated, I celebrated how well I treated had her while we were friends. I was damn good to her. I was happy with how I was managing my response to this problem, compared to the one years before. Lastly, I lifted myself all the way up. I looked at the wonderful woman I had become over the last few years and scoffed at the thought that anyone would be so foolish to not value me more. I remembered that I am, and was, an amazing person who cared without reserve and loved without expectation.

I don't do anything for anyone with the anticipation of reciprocation. Everything that I gave her was earnest, it was pure, and I love that I can say that. Whatever happened, it wasn't all about me. She was either never really that invested or my usefulness to her ran out. Whichever the case, it reflects her and her toxic journey. At the bare minimum, we have two different definitions of what friendship looks like, how conflict resolution occurs, and what constitutes a healthy way to treat one another. For that reason alone, I knew this wasn't a relationship I needed to fight for. I now know myself well enough to confirm that this isn't a healthy space for my care to reside. I have no hard feelings. I don't waste emotion that way anymore.

PUSH FORWARD

I started this book because I felt like a failure. I felt toxic to anyone my heart touched. I wasn't treating myself well. My relationships with my closest friends weren't where I wanted them to be, and I needed to figure out what was going on.

What happened to me?

What happened to them?

What happened to us?

Can we fix this?

After hours of conversations with women, it began to make sense. We weren't failing. We were stopping in all the wrongs places. Instead of requiring more from ourselves, we stopped personal development, didn't prioritize purposeful self-love, and instead looked outward for justification.

Which easier milestones can I reach?

What else can I buy?

This is just the way I am.

Instead of being in the best friendships by growing with one another, we stopped and settled for whatever we could get.

But we've been friends so long.

All I need is my family anyway.

As long as I have someone to club with.

Instead of seeking and working toward new connections with a new community of women, we stopped in order to prevent ourselves from being hurt.

I like to keep my circle small.

All women are the same anyway.

I've been down that road before.

We have so many excuses about why we don't need to keep going, start growing, and try glowing. Stopping is making and keeping us toxic. We can't stop; we have to push forward.

I have been working continuously, tirelessly, and without fail on this book and on myself since 2012. I've fallen in love with the challenge of being a better person to other women, but more importantly, being the best friend to myself. That is why my last toxic story is so different from my first. That is why I'm so confident that what I am telling you can improve your life. I have seen it first hand. I can pinpoint when a relationship begins to become unhealthy. I can recognize when I am not in my ideal emotional state. I believe in fine-tuning my internal masterpiece, with detail paid to reviewing my motivations before anyone else's actions. At this point, thankfully, I pat myself on the back more than I kick myself in the ass. But when I do mess up, I don't stop at the mistake. I push forward.

Words before actions lead to greater satisfaction. Declaring your intent is just as important as doing the work to accomplish your goal. If you are not purposeful in using your words to guide your actions and maintain your motivation, you are not healing from the inside out. As you progress, keep talking to yourself. That running dialog matters.

Practice looking inward so much that it becomes second nature. You should also be the first person you analyze when a relationship goes awry. When you get in the habit of emotional conditioning, you quickly understand that critiquing does not have to be negative. When you tune into yourself, you will naturally seek to beautify the spaces you occupy with a less toxic outlook. Your revitalized personal health, and your renewed friendship with yourself, will drive you toward better and more authentic connections. If you encounter a time when you feel your efforts are in vain, don't let doubt stop you, push forward.

Investment in your happiness is the most significant energy you can expend. Everything you do begins and ends with the quality of what you have given to yourself. But, you still have to deal with other women in your life. Every personality I have defined and every tip I have given to best interact with them will assist you in keeping your new investment safe. When you are faced with a situation that feels beyond your ability, don't stop, utilize your new resources, see the situation with a refreshed vision, operate with strength, and push forward.

The work you put in matters. Being a healthier woman and living your least toxic life revolves around being your own best friend and propelling yourself from that point. Never stop. Always. Push. Forward.

Thank you for taking this chance on yourself. Feel free to tell the world, "You're welcome," every step of the way.

ACKNOWLEDGEMENTS

I must begin by thanking my amazing husband, Jaron. You've always believed in me more than I believed in myself. Your support, from reading every word I write to taking care of our Littles while I am working, is why this book is finished. I love and appreciate you beyond words.

To my friends and family, thank you for giving me advice and support throughout this entire process. You guys never let me give up, even when I tried. I owe you so much.

Thank you to the many women that opened their hearts and shared their stories with me. I did not know where I was going with this book until your experiences humbled, motivated, and directed me.

A special thank you to Debra and Shannon for working with me throughout the editing process. Your guidance and patience refined my vision into a book I am proud to present. Thank you, Ashley, for not just designing my awesome cover, but doing so when you had so much on your plate.

Thank you to The Metaphor Club for providing the ideal creative space for me to grow as a writer. Without your welcoming environment and abundant coffee, I would still be *trying* to write this book.

In all my years of writing, I never thought my first book would be a nonfiction. But this subject spoke to me so loud and clear, it would not allow me to move on until I gave it the voice it demanded.

Thank you for taking the time to read my book. It has been a journey for me as a woman and a writer.

I appreciate you growing with me.

Made in the USA
San Bernardino,
CA